Remember the fanatical, close-minded religious zealots from *Inherit the Wind?*

They're back.

*... They've just changed sides.*

"*Troubled House* is a terrific play! Many have dreamed of rewriting *Inherit the Wind* to take account of the fact that Darwinism is now the entrenched orthodoxy that is troubling its own house by imposing thought control on science. The trick is to make the reworked drama as exciting and entertaining as the original. Daniel Schwabauer has accomplished that, and I think audiences will love his drama. I hope it has many, many performances."

*- Phillip E. Johnson, author of <u>Darwin on Trial</u>*

"Daniel Schwabauer has a rare talent for putting his finger on the heart of hypocrisy. *Troubled House* is a timely reminder that intolerance is not exclusive to religion--and that naturalistic philosophy masquerading as science has become the new orthodoxy. Teachers who truly want to challenge students to think independently will find *Troubled Hous*e inspiring and challenging."

*- Professor Mark Wilson,*
*Southwestern Oregon Community College*

# TROUBLED HOUSE

### by Daniel Schwabauer

"He that troubleth his own house ...
Shall inherit the wind."

AUTHORS NOTE:

Although the ramifications of the science involved in this play are inevitably con-
tentious, I have tried to remain neutral regarding the question of human origins. It
is my hope that *Troubled House* be read and performed with this same neutrality in
mind. The play neither promotes - nor defends - any religious (nor anti-religious)
ideology regarding Darwin's theory of evolution.

**Interested in launching a production of *Troubled House*?**

For pricing of playbooks, performance application or other information, contact the
author at:

dan@troubledhouse.com

or visit the website at:

www.troubledhouse.com

Clear Water Press
PO Box 62
Olathe, KS 66051
www.clearwaterpress.com

ISBN: 0-9742972-0-8

First printing 2003.

Cover design by CDS Creative Design.
www.cdscreativedesign.com

Printed in the United States of America

# TROUBLED HOUSE

# The CHARACTERS:

ORSON KEYES, Prof. of Biology. Middle-aged. Physically unremarkable, but possessing a keen intellect and a passion for truth. He neither cares what people think of him nor understands why he should.

TESS DeSILVA, Prof. of English, and ORSON's girlfriend, also middle-aged, though perhaps a few years younger. She is the one most irritated by ORSON's dedication to the truth, and the one who most admires him for it.

RODNEY HARRIS, graduate student and reporter for the student newspaper, The Springdale Daily. Early twenties. Cynical, brash, arrogant.

SCOTT TATE, student editor of *The Springdale Daily*.

MARGARET CRIPPIN, Dean of the University. Late fifties. Severe, humorless, Chair of the Board of Inquiry.

WILLEM SCHURHOLZ, Professor Emeritus, Dean of the College of Life Sciences. Middle sixties, and very near retirement, though he is not the sort of man to give up work willingly. The thought of some day leaving the university depresses him. He is ORSON's mentor and most vocal detractor.

DAVID BOOKNIGHT, Dean of the College of Religious Studies. Late forties, a closet atheist fond of platitudes equating Nature with God and vice versa. Dresses in a clerical collar.

COREY VAUGHN, Professor of Mathematics. Middle-aged and soft-spoken.

Reporters Cynthia TANNER and Luis ESPANOZA

Television news ANCHOR and his CAMERA PERSON

The newspaper DELIVERY PERSON

Todd PARKER and various other STUDENTS

# ACT 1 ONE

The
## SETTING


*The campus of an ivy-league university, the present. Upstage, the campus lawn overlooks the lower stage from a raised platform. A large sign reading, "Springdale University" overshadows the stage. In the background around the lawn are the Library and the various buildings. Upstage right stands a door to the School of Journalism, above which is inscribed: "The Truth shall make you free." This should be kept visible through the course of the play. Opposite that, upstage left, stands the door to the College of Natural Sciences. Upstage center is a covered gazebo.*

*The conference room and office space, downstage center and left, consists of a desk and chair, and a large conference table with four chairs.*

*The editorial office of the* Springdale Daily, *downstage right, is a chaotic mess. SCOTT Tate's desk is cluttered with papers, books, Mountain Dew cans, Starbuck's coffee cups, a soiled coffee pot, a telephone, and a computer.*

*The third wall, separating the campus lawn from both rooms, is invisible.*

ACT I


Scene 1


*The lights come up on SCOTT Tate, downstage right, who is busily typing at his computer. Behind him, the campus lawn is barely visible in the moonlight. It is now late evening.*

*SCOTT makes a final entry, runs his hands through his hair, and reaches for the phone.*

SCOTT
(*dialing*)

Kilgore? I just emailed the file. Can you hold off on printing the front page?

(*Looking at his watch*)

I don't know, twenty minutes?

(*Listening*)


(*RODNEY Harris bursts onto the campus lawn, upstage left, in a hurry to reach the Journalism Building. He carries a briefcase. Halfway across the lawn he trips, the briefcase opens, its contents spill out: papers, books, etc. He jams the items back into the case, smashing it down to get it closed, and then hurries to the door of the Journalism Building. He exits.*)

SCOTT
(*cont.*)

One of my reporters called in with a hot story.

(*pause*)

He wouldn't tell me over the phone. Just said it was good versus evil, right versus wrong, and Yankees versus Red Sox.

(*pause*)

Yeah, it was Rodney. Sounds like he's got something on the administration again.

(*pause*)

Thanks.

(*SCOTT hangs up, pushes back his chair, and starts to pace in front of his desk. He looks at his watch again and mutters to himself.*)

(*RODNEY enters through the office door. He is out of breath, but he composes himself, trying to appear nonchalant, and plunks his case down on the desk.*)

SCOTT
(*looking at his watch - again*)
You said ten minutes.

RODNEY
You'll want to kiss me when you hear this.

SCOTT
You're quitting?

RODNEY
I graduate in two weeks.

SCOTT
(*Returning to his seat, he conceals his interest by typing on the keyboard.*)
That's not a story - that's a miracle.

RODNEY
Funny. You know, you're getting awfully cocky for an undergraduate. Have you forgotten that used to be my chair?

SCOTT
Tried to and failed. What's this story?

RODNEY
(*Smiling. He smells SCOTT's curiosity.*)
Scandal.

SCOTT
(*after a pause - he is no longer typing.*)
I'm listening.

RODNEY

We play this right and the syndicates will be lining up to hire us when we graduate.

SCOTT
(*after another pause*)
You *are* windy when you want to be.

RODNEY
(*delaying, enjoying the suspense*)
Yes, sir. We have a story to write. Time to wake up and smell the coffee.
(*RODNEY lifts the coffee pot, sniffs cautiously at the lid, then wrinkles his nose as he sets it down.*)
Or not.

SCOTT
(*shaking his head - he begins to type again.*)
I don't have time for this, Rodney!

RODNEY
(*indicating the computer*)
What are you working on?
(*He comes around behind the desk so that he can see the monitor.*)
Another bleeding-heart column for the tree huggers?

SCOTT
It's Faulkner. A term paper on *The Sound and the Fury.*

RODNEY
(*He reads a few lines over SCOTT's shoulder and shakes his head.*)
For Pete's sake, Scott, you're an English major. You're supposed to be good at English.

SCOTT
We've all got our weaknesses. What's the story? You kill somebody?

RODNEY
Better than murder. (*grandly*) Sleepy Springdale shocks students, suspends scholar.

SCOTT
(*unimpressed*)
I called Kilgore for that? He says you're a pinhead, by the way.

RODNEY
(*Rapping loudly on the desktop with his knuckles*)
What's this?

SCOTT

Annoying.

RODNEY
(*RODNEY puts his arm around SCOTT's shoulders. His tone is
that of an older brother, a mentor, a visionary exercising great
patience with one of the unenlightened.*)
It's opportunity knocking, Scott. This story will make me famous, and
I'm going to bring you along for the ride. That's the kind of friend I am.

SCOTT
I know what kind of friend you are. Leave me out.

RODNEY
When parents get wind of this they'll panic. They'll pull their kids out
of here so fast it'll make Dean Crippin's wig fall off.

SCOTT
(*skeptical*)
And send them where? To a State university? I don't think so.

RODNEY
(*undaunted*)
Crusty old alums - businessmen who wear Springdale Rolexes and
smoke cigars as they drink Stoli on the back nine - will inhale the stink
of incompetence all the way to their Wall street ivory towers. You know
what that will do to the school's research coffers?
    (*SCOTT is starting to get interested now, and RODNEY can
    feel it. RODNEY loves having an audience, even of one.*)
We put this on our web-site and we'll have more hits than Dick Clark.
CNN will come to me--to us--for information. Think of it, Scott! You
want sound and fury? Our story will rattle this suffocating old ivy-
league cage faster than you can say "Pulitzer Prize."

SCOTT
(*intrigued*)

Why?  Who's getting the axe?

RODNEY
(*drawing it out*)

Professor - Orson - Keyes.

SCOTT

The biology teacher?  (*suddenly skeptical*) Oh, I get it.  He's the one who flunked you your freshman year.

RODNEY

Vengeance has nothing to do with it.  The problem is what he's spouting to the little darlings in his classes.

SCOTT

Keyes is brilliant.  His Biology text is used all across the country.  What did he do?

RODNEY
(*smugly*)

He got religion.

SCOTT
(*after a pause*)

I don't believe it.

RODNEY

Neither do I.  But our readers will.

SCOTT

So what is he?  A Jehova's Witness?  A Hare Krishna?

RODNEY

Worse.

SCOTT

A born-again Christian?

RODNEY

Keyes says he's not sure about evolution anymore.

SCOTT
(*incredulous*)

He's a Creationist?


RODNEY

That's the spin we're going to put on it.


SCOTT

Don't give me spin.  Is he, or isn't he?


RODNEY

Well, technically speaking, he isn't.  He's more of a bull-dog skeptic.
The unfashionable kind, with more honesty than tact.  He suffers from
the delusion that his job is to present every side of every issue.


SCOTT

Even on evolution?


RODNEY

He promotes doubt better than an election year bill-board.


SCOTT

Okay, so he's irritating.  Where's the story in that?


RODNEY
(*slyly*)

Any story is what you make of it.


SCOTT

But you just said this was big -


RODNEY

I said it *will* be big.  After we're through with it.  Remember those cute
freshmen girls we met last night at the Beta Party?


SCOTT

How could I forget?


RODNEY
(*Grinning*)

All four of them have Keyes for Freshman Biology.

SCOTT

So what's the story?

RODNEY
(*patiently*)

The story is that he's giving answers. The *wrong* answers. They all filled out an evaluation on Keyes yesterday.

SCOTT
(*understanding*)

Ahhhh.

RODNEY

That's just the beginning. One whiff of this and Dean Crippin will have to conduct a hearing. We'll have front-page ammo until school's out for the semester.

SCOTT
(*considering*)

No. (*firmly*) We can't do it.

RODNEY
(*surprised*)

Whaddaya mean, can't?

SCOTT

This is a newspaper, Rodney. We report facts. We don't create them.

RODNEY

Says the Boy Scouts? Nobody spews that drivel any more. You ever watch the nightly news?

SCOTT

I like being able to live with myself in the morning.

RODNEY

That's never been a problem for me.

SCOTT

I believe you.

RODNEY

You want a merit badge or a story? I didn't tell them what to write on their evaluations.  I just gave them some advice about wording.

                              SCOTT
                       (*weighing the facts*)
And they did it?

                              RODNEY
    (*He opens his briefcase, shuffles the contents, withdraws several
    pieces of paper, and hands them to SCOTT.*)
I have exact copies of all four.  I asked the girls to make duplicates after
class.

                              SCOTT
                    (*reading it with interest*)
Word for word?

                              RODNEY
Close enough.
                              SCOTT
                          (*impressed*)
This could be huge.

                              RODNEY
Dean Crippin won't know what to do with Keyes when she reads tomorrow's edition.

                              SCOTT
She'll either have to pat his back or flog it.

                              RODNEY
                     (*enjoying the words*)
I'm going to make a whip.

                              SCOTT
And so much for the truth.
    (*As though making up his mind.*)
No, Rodney.  We can't do this.

                              RODNEY
                    (*pretending to give in*)
Okay.  I guess you're right.

*(SCOTT is shocked into silence by Rodney's surrender.*
*RODNEY begins to examine his fingernails. After a pause:)*
By the way, what's the big scoop in tomorrow's gossip column?

SCOTT
(exploding)

We have to be accurate!

RODNEY

By printing that stuff about him being a truth-seeker? That won't work! It doesn't fit anyone's pre-conceived bias. No one will understand. No one will care. Worst of all, no one will read about it.

SCOTT
(dryly)

Which would mean no national media, no cameras, no mortified parents to put your name in the spotlight.

RODNEY

To put *our* names in the spotlight.

SCOTT

Springdaily Scoops Newsweek.

RODNEY
(amicably)

We owe it to ourselves, Scott. We owe it to our future as journalists. And we owe it to our readers.

SCOTT

It *would* be nice to print something juicy for once.

RODNEY

Enter Professor Keyes!

*(Orson KEYES enters upstage left from the College of Natural Sciences. He is a plain-looking man, not particularly handsome or charismatic. He closes the door behind him and glances at his watch. He takes a cell phone from his pocket and dials.)*

Bible-thumper.  Creationist.  Right-wing, born-again fundamentalist.
*(enthusiastically, almost to himself, almost as though
before a multitude.)*
A man who tries to foist the Genesis story on a flock of eager, unsuspecting college kids.  A man who doesn't deserve the distinction of being called a scientist, much less a professor.

KEYES

Hi, honey.  I'm leaving now, but I'll be late.

*(KEYES puts the phone back in his pocket and exits, upstage right.)*

SCOTT

With your talent for spin, Rodney, you should have been a spider.

RODNEY
*(taking this as a compliment.)*

Maybe you can learn something from me.
  *(picking up his case)*
Come on.  Let's get some java.  We can hammer out the first page on my laptop and email it to Kilgore by midnight.  Tomorrow morning I'll show you how to push newsprint the old-fashioned way.

SCOTT
*(They pause at the door for a moment)*

Are you sure you've thought this through?  What if something unexpected happens?

RODNEY

Haven't I taught you anything, Scott?  It's not what happens that really matters.  It's how you *describe* it.

*(RODNEY and SCOTT exit.)*

Scene 2

*Morning, the next day.  The lights come up softly over the campus, suggesting dawn.  A DELIVERY PERSON enters carrying a bundle of wrapped newspapers, which he deposits outside the door of the Journalism Building.  He exits.*

(*RODNEY and SCOTT enter upstage right.*)

RODNEY

The problem is getting them to read it. Two semesters of that luke-warm milk you've been serving would put anyone to sleep.
   (*Pointing to the papers*)
Right on time.

(*They go to the bundle of papers and cut it loose.*)

SCOTT

Morning classes should be over right about ... (*he looks at his watch*) ... now.

(*STUDENTS begin to cross the campus lawn. They generally ignore SCOTT's attempt to hawk papers. A few reluctantly take the papers he's handing out, but don't express real interest. RODNEY stands back for a moment and watches SCOTT's technique.*)

Get your papers here! Free Sprindale Daily! Get 'em while they're hot, people! What about you? No? You? That's more like it. Special edition here! Springdale Daily!

RODNEY
(*shaking his head as he approaches*)
That's no way to push newsprint.

SCOTT
(*stubbornly*)
I suppose you could do better. Papers here! Special edition, absolutely free! Don't wait for the afternoon edition!

RODNEY
(*He climbs the gazebo and speaks in a commanding tone, full of self-assurance and patient urgency. He is selling something that he knows they want: a story.*)
Scandal - rocks - Springdale - Biology - Department! Read all about it! Scandal threatens research!
   (*He points to a passing STUDENT [#1]*)
Hey you!

(*But STUDENT #1 is in a hurry and ignores him. Another STUDENT [#2] responds.*)

STUDENT #2

Who, Me?

RODNEY

Yes! You know Professor Keyes?

STUDENT #2

Never heard of him.

RODNEY

Biology 101, been here six years.

STUDENT #2
(*losing interest*)

I've gotta go.

RODNEY

Take a paper with you!
  (*STUDENT #2 approaches impatiently and RODNEY hands over
  a paper.*)
Read about it while you're sitting in class. Give you something important to think about: Freedom of thought!
  (*STUDENT #2 slows his exit, reading carefully. As RODNEY says
  these last three words, STUDENT #2 returns to listen, clearly
  worried.*)

STUDENT #3

I've heard of Keyes. What about him?

RODNEY

The paper is calling for a board of inquiry to decide whether he should
be fired for what he's teaching as science.

STUDENT #3

Aw, so what?
  (*He starts to leave*)

RODNEY
(*antagonizing him*)

I suppose your mummy and daddy paid your tuition. What do you care about the separation of Church and State?...

STUDENT #3
(*turning angrily*)
I'm on a scholarship, you moron. I earned my way here!

(*A few students are starting to take an interest in the commotion; they begin to take papers from SCOTT and RODNEY, but warily.*)

RODNEY
Moron, huh? So you think teachers should have the right to force their religious opinions onto their students?

STUDENT #3
(*suspiciously*)
No.

RODNEY
Give tests on how many animals Moses put on the ark?

STUDENT #4
Is that what he's doing?

SCOTT
(*suddenly inspired*)
Creationist teacher bashes evolution in class! Says Adam and Eve rode dinosaurs! Read aaalll about it!

(*Student #4 takes the paper and begins to read.*)

STUDENT #4
Look at this! (*yelling across the campus*) Hey, Parker! Check this out!

(*More students are beginning to gather around RODNEY. SCOTT is passing out papers as fast as he can.*)

RODNEY
(*dramatically*)
The Springdaily is calling for an investigation. But so far, Dean Crippin has not responded on whether Keyes will be kept on the faculty.

STUDENT #4
(*indignantly*)
They re going to let him keep his job?

RODNEY
Looks like it.  In spite of these allegations.

STUDENT #5
(*holding up a paper*)
But this is a violation of our civil rights.

STUDENT #3
Didn't I hear this Keyes guy is a real bible-thumper?

STUDENT #5
That figures!  Next thing you know we'll have mandatory prayer meetings in the chapel.

RODNEY
(*mockingly*)
Let me hear you say Amen to that, Brothers and Sisters!

STUDENT #6
Amen!

PARKER
What's going on?

STUDENT #4
(*pointing to the paper*)
Says some biology professor is preaching in class.  Wants to start mandatory prayer meetings on campus.

RODNEY
Let me hear you say, Praise the Lord!

PARKER
He can't do that.

STUDENT #6
Praise the Lord!

STUDENT #7
Hallelujah!

SCOTT
Amen!

STUDENT #5
Don't bet on it!

RODNEY
Springdale used to have mandatory church services in the 1920s. You never know what religious zealots will do!

(*The students are gathering into a mob now. Some of them protest as they read, and more students pour in as the commotion piques their curiosity.*)

PARKER
(*Looking at a paper*)
Wait a minute. Orson Keyes? This can't be true. I had this guy my Freshman year and he never said this stuff.

STUDENT #8
Says evolution may not be true?!?

STUDENT #9
Genesis story gives true picture of human origins?

STUDENT #10
Darwin is burning in hell! Do you believe this stuff?

PARKER
(*His voice is lost among the outrage*)
But he wouldn't have said those things!

STUDENT #5
Isn't this the same guy who says the Earth is only six thousand years old?

STUDENT #7
Hey Rodney! What's the deal with this religious nut?

RODNEY

Now you know I'm not the editor of the school paper any more. Scott here is the one who's done the research. And you can read all about it -

STUDENT #8

Come on, Rodney, tell us what's going on!

RODNEY

Wait a minute! I have my journalistic integrity to think of.

STUDENT #5

Is Dean Crippin really going to let this Keyes bozo keep his job?

RODNEY

You want the honest truth?

STUDENT #7

Let's hear it!

STUDENT #8

Tell us!

STUDENT #9

Come on, Rodney!

RODNEY

(*Allowing himself to be persuaded - with no apparent regret - RODNEY spreads his hands out for quiet. The mayhem temporarily subsides.*)

We all came to Springdale for just two reasons: Cheap beer ...

(*The crowd whoops*)

... and an education. On the first count I have no complaints.

(*Someone claps STUDENT #3 on the back, and there are more cheers.*)

But listen.

(*RODNEY's tone grows more serious*)

Two days ago, *The SpringDaily* began investigating rumors that Professor Orson Keyes has been teaching controversial - and possibly unconstitutional - religious beliefs in the classroom.

(*The crowd boos, hisses, begins to murmur angrily.*)

The paper is calling for a Board of Inquiry to conduct hearings on the allegations that Professor Keyes is teaching that the theory of evolution -

STUDENT #7

Good God, it's true!


STUDENT #5

He can't teach this stuff at a federally funded institution!  I'm a law student.  I know this stuff.


STUDENT #7
(*shouting*)

Professor Keyes is a religious fool!


STUDENT #9
(*shouting back*)

Tell him to go thump his Bible somewhere else!


SCOTT
(*inspired - to the crowd*)

Orson Keyes thinks You're a Fool!


STUDENT #8

HE'S the Fool!


STUDENT #5

Fire Keyes!


SCOTT
(*chanting*)

Wants the Bible Taught in School!


STUDENT #9

Tell him to keep his religion to himself!


SCOTT

Orson Keyes thinks you're a fool!  Wants the Bible Taught in School!


(*The crowd demonstrates its wrath with a mixture of boos and cheers.  They begin to chant together, slowly at first, then with more rhythm and volume.  Their voices rise in unison.*)


STUDENTS

ORSON KEYES THINKS YOU'RE A FOOL!

WANTS THE BIBLE TAUGHT IN SCHOOL!
ORSON KEYES THINKS YOU'RE A FOOL!
WANTS THE BIBLE TAUGHT IN SCHOOL!


RODNEY
(*As the crowd's venom swells, RODNEY has to shout to be heard above them.*)
- as I said, Keyes allegedly stated that the theory of evolution may not be true ...-


(*The crowd's anger crescendos, its litany repeated over and over mindlessly. The students are enjoying themselves. But RODNEY can no longer be heard. He turns to SCOTT, who is watching from the fringes. SCOTT shrugs, palms held up. RODNEY smiles broadly and holds up one thumb.*)


(*lights out*)


Scene 3


*Dawn, a few days later. It is the morning of the inevitable hearing. KEYES enters, apparently lost in thought. He does not seem to be going anywhere in particular. He wears a coat and tie now, and looks uncomfortable doing so. He stops, hands on his hips, and stares at the Natural Sciences Building as though searching for something.*


KEYES
(*to himself.*)
The question isn't *could it happen?* but *did it happen?* Consider stone on stone. Complexity. Organization. Windows and doors. Pipes bring fresh water and emit waste. Filters scrub the air. And crowning it all, etched above the door -

*(TESS DeSILVA enters upstage right. She is a picture of the
professional woman, a literature professor with a kind face. Just
now she is uncharacteristically nervous.)*

- placed as though on purpose, and hinting that knowledge itself represents some higher absolute -

TESS

Orson!

KEYES
*(turning)*

Tess! What are you doing here?

TESS
*(relieved)*

When I woke up and you weren't next to me I thought - I don't know. I
was worried about you. About the hearing.

KEYES

I just wanted some time to think. I like to walk the campus at sunrise.

TESS
*(looking around at the empty campus, as though seeing it
for the first time.)*

I suppose you *can* really think here when no one else is around.

KEYES

And not at all when they are.

TESS

Feels different when it's empty.

KEYES

Later in the day there are too many people. Like a crowd of insects.
Always in a hurry, always so sure of where they're going. Sometimes I
envy them.

TESS

It's an act, Orson. They don't know where they're going any more than
you and I do.

KEYES

What's that supposed to mean?

TESS

If you'd get to know them better you'd realize that the point is not to get anywhere in particular, but to keep moving. Take marriage as an example.

KEYES

What does knowing them have to do with natural law? An object in motion tends to stay in motion until acted upon by some other force. And I'm not ready yet.

TESS

Inside, they're terrified. When, do you think?

KEYES

Terrified of what?

TESS

Standing still.

KEYES
(*looking at her*)
It's strange, the things that frighten us.

TESS
(*insistently*)
When?

KEYES
(*awkwardly*)
When I've thought it through.

TESS

We've been living together for two years. Aren't we compatible?

KEYES

Made for each other.

TESS

Then what's to think about?

KEYES

Are you kidding? Everything! Kids, careers, the origin of life. Your mother.

TESS
(*exasperated*)

Just once can't you act on what you *feel* instead of what you *think*?

KEYES
(*gently*)

My students tell me what they feel every day. They feel they aren't getting enough individual attention. They feel their grades are unfair. No one says, *I think* anymore. It's always, *I feel*. You know why? Because you can't criticize a feeling. You can't say that someone's feelings are wrong.

TESS

How about nonexistent?

KEYES

The problem with feelings is that they are too - too easy.

TESS

Oh, really? Then you should be able to tell me how you feel about me.

KEYES
(*hesitating*)

I - want to be sure of things.

TESS

No one is sure of things. We do the best we can with what we have.

(*KEYES takes hold of her shoulders gently and stares into her eyes for a moment. His expression might be love, it might be doubt. After a long moment she realizes he is not going to say it, and she pulls away.*)

TESS

Forget it.

KEYES

Tess, it's not that I don't love you, it's just that -

TESS

Love is over-rated anyway.
(*She relents. She has known him for a long time and does not expect him to change, though she can't stop trying.*)
Look at you. You're wearing a tie.

KEYES

(*He looks down at it; he seems to have forgotten about it.*)
Do you think I should take it off? It feels so -- artificial.

TESS

(*she straightens it for him*)
The *purpose* of a tie is artificiality. Don't you know that, Orson? It hides your neck and covers your heart. It conceals your vulnerabilities. That's why men wear them to places like church. That's why you should keep it on at the hearing. In fact, it needs to be tightened.
(*She pulls the knot tighter.*)

KEYES

That's *too* tight.

TESS

It looks good.

KEYES

(*he loosens it*)
Besides, I don't have anything to hide.

TESS

That's the kind of thing that worries me. Everyone has something to hide, whether they know it or not. Orson, you really should have a law-yer with you. This hearing is more serious than you think.

KEYES

I've told you, I can't afford an attorney.

TESS

My mother always said that the only thing more expensive than a good lawyer -

KEYES

- is not having one at all. We've been through this. And your mother is in prison.

                              TESS

See? She ought to know.


                              KEYES

This isn't a trial. It's just a hearing. Dean Crippin wants to know what
really happened, and I'm going to tell her. I'm not afraid of the truth.


                              TESS

Well, you should be. You'd have more friends.


                              KEYES

I don't want those kinds of friends.
      (*He takes her by the arm and leads her to the JOURNALISM
      building.*)
Look. What do you see?


                              TESS
                            (*staring*)

A building.


                              KEYES

More specific.


                              TESS
                           (*shrugging*)

The journalism building.


                              KEYES

And above the door? The inscription?


                              TESS

Don't be patronizing, Orson. I'm a full professor, not one of your students.


                              KEYES

Of course not.


                              TESS

Because I hate it when you're patronizing.


                              KEYES

What does it say?

TESS
(*she sighs and reads disinterestedly*)
"The Truth shall make you free."

KEYES
Yes. What do you think it means?

TESS
It's from the Bible. A fossil from the victorian period, when Springdale was a missionary college.

KEYES
But what does it mean?

TESS
(*shrugging*)
I suppose it implies that if you know the truth, people can't control you.

KEYES
What do you think, Tess? Is it just religious pap?

TESS
It's a nice saying, that's all. It looks good etched in stone. Latin poetry looks good in stone, too. So does "Rest in Peace." Don't tell me you found God out here in the sunrise.

KEYES
I haven't found anything. I just - I want the right to keep looking.

TESS
And the right to make everyone else look, too? Why do you have to keep pushing them, Orson?

KEYES
All I want is to ask questions. What's so wrong with that?

(*RODNEY and SCOTT enter upstage left, then stop abruptly when they see KEYES and TESS standing together with their backs towards them. RODNEY points.*)

SCOTT
Is that him?

                              TESS

Sometimes you have to just let go.


                             KEYES

Let go of the truth?


                            RODNEY

Speak of the devil.


                             SCOTT

So *that's* what he looks like.


                              TESS
                         (*after a pause*)

... Yes.


                            RODNEY
                          (*to SCOTT*)

Well. (*shrugging*) Carpe Diem.


                             KEYES

Without the truth, what would we be?


                            RODNEY
               (*approaching, holding out his hand.*)

Professor Keyes?


                              TESS

Insects.


                             KEYES
                        (*taking his hand*)

Yes.


                            RODNEY

Rodney Harris, Springdale Daily.
    (*RODNEY withdraws a pocket tape recorder from his knapsack.*)
I'd like to ask you a few questions about the hearing.


    (*SCOTT takes out a pen and pocket notepad.*)

KEYES

All right.  Perhaps you can get your facts a little straighter.

TESS
(*to RODNEY*)

Professor Keyes can't talk about it.  You'll have to speak to his attorney.

RODNEY

Attorney?

KEYES
(*shaking his head*)

I don't have an attorney.

RODNEY

Just a few questions.  What do you expect from today's hearing?

TESS
(*defensively*)

Didn't you hear what I just said?

(*RODNEY lets the question stand.  KEYES shrugs.
TESS throws her hands up and turns away in disgust.*)

KEYES

I don't know.  Questions, I guess.  You'd have to talk to Dean Crippin.

RODNEY

Any truth to the rumors that you may lose your job over your stance on creationism?

TESS
(*huffing*)

He's not teaching creationism!  Orson, tell this young man he should stick to printing football scores and columns about sexually transmitted diseases!

RODNEY
(*ignoring her*)

How about your stance on a literal interpretation of Genesis?

KEYES
(*kindly*)
I don't have a stance on Genesis. And I'm not a creationist. Look, apparently one of my students complained to the administration, and Dean Crippin thought she should look into it.

RODNEY
Is this the first time a student has complained about you?

KEYES
(*lightly*)
No, and it probably won't be the last.

RODNEY
You don't mind offending people, then?

(*Willem SCHURHOLZ enters upstage left and approaches the Natural Sciences building. He carries a briefcase. When he sees the discussion, he hesitates, starts to open the door to the Natural Sciences Building, and stops. He scratches his head, listening, then sets the briefcase down and folds his arms disapprovingly.*)

TESS
He didn't say that.

KEYES
(*to TESS*)
But I will say it!
(*to RODNEY*)
The goal of teaching is to lead your students to knowledge. Sometimes they take offense at what you teach, but that can't be avoided.

RODNEY
What about the other faculty members who complained about you? How do you explain their opposition?

KEYES
(*sputtering*)
I - I - don't know what you mean. I haven't offended any teachers! Tess?

TESS
(*rolling her eyes*)

No comment.

(*SCOTT glances back and forth at both of them, then scribbles
something furiously in his notepad, jabbing pen to paper with obvious emphasis.*)

RODNEY

So you expect to be vindicated?

SCHURHOLZ

Absolutely he'll be vindicated.

RODNEY
(*They all notice SCHURHOLZ now.  Orson is pleased to see him.*)
Professor Sherwood?

SCHURHOLZ

Schur*holz*, Rodney.  Spell it right this time if you intend to quote me
again.

KEYES
(*offering his hand*)

Willem!

SCHURHOLZ

Orson.
(*Shaking KEYES' hand, he indicates RODNEY*)
I see you've caught another snake.

KEYES

What?
(*realizing, he smiles*)
Oh.  Not really.  He just wanted to ask me a few questions about the
hearing.  I think he'll be easy to let go.

RODNEY
(*to SCHURHOLZ*)

You're on the board?

SCHURHOLZ

I am.


RODNEY
(*raising his eyebrows*)
This is an *open* hearing, isn't it?


SCHURHOLZ
Unfortunately. But seating will be limited.


TESS
Thank God
  (*They all look at her*)
... or whomever.


SCHURHOLZ
If you'll excuse us, I have an appointment with Professor Keyes.
Rodney. Scott. Ms. DeSilva.
  (*He takes KEYES by the shoulder and guides him toward the
  Natural Sciences Building.*)


KEYES
Appointment?


SCHURHOLZ
In my office.


RODNEY
But I'm not through with my interview!


SCHURHOLZ
(*over his shoulder*)
In fact, young man, you are.


TESS
Orson, I'll be a few minutes late to the hearing. I'll come after I finish
teaching my American Lit class.


RODNEY
(*to KEYES*)
I'd like to speak with you later about this, Professor Keyes!

*(KEYES and SCHURHOLZ exit into the Natural Sciences
Building. RODNEY turns to SCOTT.)*
Well, how do you like that?

SCOTT

Professor Emeritus Willem Schurholz the second. Smooth as honey. He
called you a snake, you know.

RODNEY

I'd like to teach that old fart some respect for the press.

SCOTT

But?

RODNEY

But he scares the hell out of me.
*(TESS regards RODNEY and SCOTT with utter contempt, then
turns to leave, upstage right. She tries to sneak off quietly.
RODNEY notices and starts to follow her.)*
Oh, Miss! Just a moment of your time, please -

TESS
*(emphatically)*

Oh, no!

RODNEY

I'd like to talk to you about the -

TESS
*(turning)*

Drop dead! D-E-A-D! You can quote me.
*(TESS exits, upstage right.)*

RODNEY
*(letting the words fall into silence)*

- about the hearing.

SCOTT

Why are these professors so touchy today?

RODNEY

Survival instinct. They smell the blood in the water. But they're not
sure yet which one of them is for dinner. Come on.

(*RODNEY and SCOTT exit, upstage left.*)

(*KEYES and SCHURHOLZ enter downstage left. SCHURHOLZ
closes the door behind them.*)

SCHURHOLZ

- which is why I wanted to get you away from him. But I really did
want to talk to you.

KEYES

I should know better, I guess. But really, Willem, the *SpringDaily* is just
a campus paper. It's not *Newsweek*.

SCHURHOLZ

Never underestimate the power of a lie, Orson.

KEYES
(*with conviction*)

All lies crumble eventually.

SCHURHOLZ

That's a lie, too.

KEYES

Then it will crumble.

SCHURHOLZ

You should have been something else. A lawyer maybe. Anything but a
scientist. If only you didn't have so much talent for it.

KEYES

Never could think in absolutes, could you?

SCHURHOLZ

Absolutely not.

KEYES

Tell me the truth. This isn't really about me, is it?

SCHURHOLZ

It's about nothing *but* you. Your insistence on ...
  (*motioning with his hand, searching for the right word*)
... *evidence*, or whatever you want to call it.


KEYES

I thought there might be another agenda behind this. Still, I'm glad
you'll be there today. It will be good to see a friendly face.


SCHURHOLZ
(*frowning, his voice grave*)

About that -


KEYES
(*waving him off*)

I know we don't always agree, Willem. I'm not asking you for any special favors.


SCHURHOLZ

I didn't expect you to. Have a seat.


KEYES
(*Pulls a chair in front of the desk and sits.*)

What, then?


SCHURHOLZ
(*He pulls a key ring from his pocket and unlocks the desk drawer.*)

This hearing today. It won't exactly be friendly.


KEYES
(*warily*)

Meaning?


SCHURHOLZ
(*He withdraws a half-empty liquor bottle and two glasses from the
  drawer.*)

Sterilizing alcohol. The janitor keeps dipping into my stock. He thinks I
don't notice.


KEYES

Vodka?

SCHURHOLZ

One hundred twenty proof.  A pleasant way to erase ... contamination.
   (*He unscrews the cap and pours some into each glass.*)


KEYES

I thought you were going to stop.


SCHURHOLZ

I meant to.  But when Rita left, giving this up
   (*he motions to the bottle*)
somehow didn't seem very important anymore.  Drink with me.


KEYES

I haven't had breakfast yet.


SCHURHOLZ

Then I'm serving.
   (*He drinks, emptying his glass.  He puts the lid back on and
   shoves the bottle back into the drawer.*)
Go ahead.


KEYES
   (*He leaves the glass untouched.*)
Thanks anyway.


SCHURHOLZ

I thought you might say that.
   (*He picks up the other glass and empties it, then puts both glasses
   back into the drawer.*)
Anyway, what I meant was that I'm not going to be all that friendly,
either.


KEYES

Crippin made you the prosecutor?


SCHURHOLZ

More like hangman.


KEYES

Why are you telling me this?

SCHURHOLZ

Because, as much as I despise myself for it, I sort of like you.

KEYES
(*chuckling*)

I won't tell anyone.

SCHURHOLZ

They wouldn't believe you anyway. You know, it wouldn't hurt for you to compromise during this hearing. You'll have every opportunity to vindicate yourself - as a scientist.

KEYES

Listen, Willem, I appreciate the advice, but -

SCHURHOLZ

But no thanks?

KEYES

I don't need to vindicate myself as a scientist. And I really ought to be going. I was on my way to the library.

(*KEYES starts to stand, but SCHURHOLZ reaches across the desk and grips his hand hard, holding him.*)

SCHURHOLZ

Come back.

KEYES
(*moved*)

For God's sake, I haven't gone anywhere.

SCHURHOLZ

You're a million miles from the rest of us.

KEYES

No, Willem. Just a few personal convictions.

SCHURHOLZ
(*with visible difficulty, he lets go of KEYES' hand.*)
Same thing.

(*KEYES goes to the door, numb, confused. He did not expect the day to begin this way.*)

Orson?

(*KEYES turns, waits.*)

Rita always liked you.

(*KEYES stands there for a moment. He does not know what to say. Finally he opens the door and exits. SCHURHOLZ watches him go, staring after him. Then he lets out a long slow breath and reaches for the desk drawer. He takes out the bottle and unscrews the lid.*)

*The curtain falls*

# ACT 2 TWO

ACT II


*The downstage area is now the meeting room where the hearing will take place. The office of the Springdale Daily is gone.*

*A table with four chairs sits just left of downstage center. The desk from Crippin's office has been moved, so that she can sit at the head of the Board next to the table. KEYES is seated to the right of downstage center behind a short desk. Next to him on the desk is a large stack of books. KEYES is separated from the spectators by a rope stretched between two weighted poles. A dozen or so chairs have been arranged in rows downstage right for the spectators.*

*The Board's table and chairs are higher than those of KEYES, lending the members of the Board a formal and imposing appearance. The hearing room looks strikingly like a courtroom.*


Scene 1


*The Board members are all seated. KEYES is also seated, but is leaning forward nervously. Behind him, students and teachers alike are packed into the chairs and open spaces, many of them standing, fanning themselves with folded newspapers, whispering to each other.*

*SCHURHOLZ, BOOKNIGHT, and VAUGHN listen with the solemnity of a jury as CRIPPIN reads from a prepared statement in a stern, commanding voice.*


CRIPPIN

- and you understand that this is not a trial?


KEYES

Yes.


CRIPPIN

But a formal hearing by a committee?

KEYES

Yes.


CRIPPIN

Made up of myself -
*(at the mention of their names, each nods)*
Professor Schurholz, Dean of the College of Natural Sciences, Professor
Booknight, Dean of the College of Religious Studies, and Dr. Corey Vaughn,
Associate Dean of the School of Mathematics?


KEYES

Yes.


CRIPPIN

All of whom have been designated by Springdale to investigate allegations
of your misconduct?


KEYES
*(surprised)*

Misconduct?


CRIPPIN

A legal term. Not meant to imply anything specific. *(less formally)* It's just
a word, Orson.


KEYES

Well, "evolution" is just a word, too. Yet here we are.


VOICE #1
*(From the safety of the crowd)*

Evolution is a fact!


VOICE #2

"Idiot" is just a word, too!


*(The spectators begin to talk at once until CRIPPIN overpowers
them.)*


CRIPPIN
*(Angrily - to the spectators)*
This hearing will NOT turn into a circus!

*(The words snap like a whip, and the spectators are instantly quiet. She continues calmly.)*

Anyone who cannot be quiet shall be removed.

*(To KEYES - she has lost her train of thought.)*

Professor Keyes, you were saying?

### KEYES

Misconduct.

### CRIPPIN
*(annoyed - she remembers now)*

You object to "misconduct?"

### KEYES

I thought this was a question of what I've been teaching - a question of subject matter. "Misconduct" sounds like I've been propositioning my students. Like I've been riding a motorcycle across the campus lawn.

### BOOKNIGHT

If you had, we wouldn't be here.

### CRIPPIN

All right.

*(She writes on the paper from which she has been reading.)*

- *allegations* of misconduct regarding subject matter discussed in the classroom. You understand this?

### KEYES

Yes.

### CRIPPIN

You also understand that your attendance is not an admission of culpability -

### KEYES

I was counting on that.

### CRIPPIN

- and that what we discuss here is not legally binding, but may be used by the university in determining whether or not to renew your contract?

KEYES

Yes.


CRIPPIN

Do you have anything you want to say before we get started?


KEYES

Yes.
   (*He stands*)
When I was told about this hearing, you said it was a simple matter of clearing my name.  But so far there hasn't been anything simple about it.  The school paper has accused me of teaching religious creationism.  Now you're telling me my contract may not be renewed.  For the record, should my attorney be here?


CRIPPIN
   (*She glances at SCHURHOLZ, who shrugs.*)
Do you want an attorney?


KEYES

That depends.  Are you going to fire me?


   (*The crowd buzzes, already forgetting the sting of CRIPPIN's wrath, then quiets as SCHURHOLZ begins to speak.*)


SCHURHOLZ
   (*stiffly*)
Look, Orson.  I think I speak for all of us when I say we'd like nothing better than to get this thing over with.


BOOKNIGHT
   (*lightly*)

I have a date tonight.


SCHURHOLZ

Investigate the facts, clear your record, and get you back to teaching science.


CRIPPIN

If you aren't happy with the outcome, you can always get a lawyer later.

SCHURHOLZ
(*reassuringly*)
But I'm sure it won't come to that.

KEYES
(*hesitating*)
... All right.

CRIPPIN
Professor Schurholz?

SCHURHOLZ
(*standing, shuffling through the papers before him*)
Yes.

CRIPPIN
You brought a summary of the facts?

SCHURHOLZ
(*Scratching his cheek, he raps the table top lightly with his knuckles - a nervous habit - and starts to pick up the paperwork. Then he thinks better of it and comes out from behind the table empty-handed.*)
I never could think sitting down. (*To CRIPPIN*) You mind?

CRIPPIN
Make yourself comfortable.

SCHURHOLZ
(*To KEYES. His manner is affable.*)
How long have we known each other, Orson?

KEYES
Roughly - (*thinking*) - twenty-five years.

SCHURHOLZ
As I recall, we met at Harvard the year I taught paleontology as a visiting professor.

KEYES
You agreed to work with me on my doctoral thesis. I learned a lot from you.

SCHURHOLZ

Of course you did. But what did you think of me at the time?

KEYES

I considered you my mentor. (*gently*) I still do, in fact.

SCHURHOLZ

(*Surprised at this last comment, a smile flickers across his face. He looks down.*)
I see. And at first?

KEYES

(*Hedging*)

... You ... irritated me.

SCHURHOLZ

(*smiling, with fondness*)
In fact, you called me, if I remember correctly, "an arrogant s.o.b."
(*The crowd titters. They like Schurholz, and consider Keyes a close-minded religious nut.*)

KEYES

I was hoping you'd forgotten that.

SCHURHOLZ

It's not every day that your best pupil insults you to your face. No doubt I deserved it. (*More serious now*) How long have you been teaching, Orson?

KEYES

Twenty-two years. The last six here at Springdale.

SCHURHOLZ

And how would you respond today - based on your many years of experience - if a student similarly insulted you?

KEYES

I don't know. It hasn't happened to me.

SCHURHOLZ

Does that surprise you?

KEYES

No.


SCHURHOLZ

Why? (*with a hint of irony*) You're just nicer than I am?


(*There is uncertain laughter. SCHURHOLZ might be making
light of the situation, but his voice holds an edge, like a drawn
sword.*)


KEYES
(*lightly - breaking the tension*)
I don't think anyone in this room would question that.


SCHURHOLZ

I suppose not. Truth is, students today have a different way of expressing themselves.
(*He crosses to the table and scoops up a handful of papers. He
holds them up as though to say, Exhibit A!* )
They have other alternatives. Safer ones.


KEYES
(*understanding*)
All of my students know that they can come to me in person. If I say
something they don't like they can come to my office -


SCHURHOLZ

- but, as I said, nowadays they don't need to. Why risk a lowered grade,
when they can simply fill out an anonymous evaluation that will be read
by the administration?


KEYES

Because the right thing to do is come to my office and discuss -


SCHURHOLZ

The *right* thing? When you hold all the cards?


KEYES

It's not a poker game, Willem. I'm on their side.

SCHURHOLZ

That's how they feel about it, too, I suppose?
*(He scans the papers in his hands, then takes his reading glasses out of his shirt-pocket and puts them on. He reads)*
What did you think of Professor Keyes as a teacher?  Answer: He seems knowledgeable but continually drivels -
*(he pauses for emphasis, so that the word hangs there in the silence.)*
- about design, which seems to be his code-word for the God of the Bible.
*(He selects another)*
Besides being boring, Reverend Keyes tends to inject his own personal religious beliefs into his lectures, and scold anyone who holds a different opinion.
*(Another)*
It's amazing that a modern scientist can believe dinosaurs lived contemporaneously with man.
*(Another)*
I don't understand what the age of the Earth has to do with molecular biology -

KEYES

*(He has been growing more and more agitated as SCHURHOLZ reads.  At last he stands.  Interrupting:)*
No student of mine could possibly have written such tripe! This is ludicrous!  I have never discussed my religious beliefs in class!

SCHURHOLZ

*(Trying to draw him out, they speak at the same time.)*
And just what are your religious beliefs, professor?

KEYES

Nor have I taught anything about the age of the Earth!

SCHURHOLZ

But you admit that you have religious beliefs that could color your analysis and your research as a scientist.

KEYES

I admit no such thing!

SCHURHOLZ

(*exploding furiously - his voice overpowers every other sound, hammers KEYES to submission*)

Then why did these students complain - in writing - that you have used the classroom to brain-wash them into accepting biblical creationism? And these are just the ones who spoke up. Who knows how many said nothing for fear of what you might do to them!

KEYES

(*He stares in silence for a moment as SCHURHOLZ's anger dissipates. Then he says softly, incredulously*)

*Do* to them, Willem?

SCHURHOLZ

(*He takes off his glasses and puts them back in his pocket.*)

Orson.

KEYES

(*unbelieving, he sits*)

What on earth could I do to them?

SCHURHOLZ

(*He slaps the papers down on the desk in front of CRIPPIN and speaks to the board*)

We all make our share of student enemies. But this is extraordinary.

VAUGHN

(*to SCHURHOLZ*)

Just how many negative evaluations do we have?

SCHURHOLZ

(*reluctantly*)

It's not the amount that matters.

VAUGHN

What, twenty? (*pause*) Ten? (*pause*) Five?

SCHURHOLZ

(*glaring coldly at VAUGHN*)

What matters is the seriousness of the accusations.

                         KEYES
                      (*recovering*)
May I see those evaluations?


                         CRIPPIN
You may not.


                         KEYES
                      (*surprised*)
No?


                         CRIPPIN
Professor Keyes, you know very well that when we ask students to complete these evaluations we promise them complete anonymity.


                         KEYES
Well, the names of the students must not be written on the evaluations,
then.


                         CRIPPIN
  (*hesitating, she doesn't bother to look at the papers*)
... No, they are not.


                         KEYES
Then where's the harm?


                         CRIPPIN
                      (*reaching*)
You might ... you might be able to ... to identify them by the handwrit-
ing.


                         KEYES
Let me see if I understand this correctly.
  (*He stands slowly and takes off his coat.*)
I am accused of using the classroom to teach biblical creationism.
Something that I have repeatedly denied -
  (*He turns slowly to look into the faces of the spectators seated
  behind him*)
- and which no person in this room has ever seen me do.  The accusa-
tions are supposedly contained in these student evaluations, which I am
not allowed to see.  The students didn't sign their names, so no one, not

                         —| 55 |—

even you, knows who actually wrote them.   My career depends on how well I defend myself in this matter.  But how can I reply to accusations I'm not allowed to read?  Or witnesses I can't question?

CRIPPIN

This is not a court of law Professor Keyes.

KEYES
(*sitting*)

I'm beginning to understand that, Dean Crippin.

SCHURHOLZ

It is not your place to question this administration!  Nor to give us lectures on the shortcomings of the system!

KEYES

I wouldn't dream of lecturing you on that topic, Willem.   You are manipulating those short-comings beautifully on your own.

SCHURHOLZ
(*furiously*)

How *dare* you accuse me?

KEYES
(*calmly*)

Would you rather I put it in writing?

CRIPPIN

Willem, please lower your voice.

SCHURHOLZ
(*loudly*)

I wasn't raising it!

CRIPPIN
(*to Keyes*)

Professor Keyes, I will not tolerate belligerence.

VAUGHN
(*looking for a compromise*)

Maybe we ought to get to the heart of the matter.  What do we expect from Professor Keyes?  In terms of his exoneration?

BOOKNIGHT
(*smugly*)
If this is a religious issue, I'd like to hear where Orson stands.  He seems to have more information than I do.

SCHURHOLZ
(*slowly, with deliberation*)
This is not about religion.  It's about science.  The issue is whether or not Springdale should tolerate philosophy being taught in a science classroom.

KEYES
Philosophy?  You don't even know what I've been teaching.  Unless you intend to accept these evaluations as proof.

SCHURHOLZ
(*facing KEYES*)
All right then, Orson.
    (*He comes over to KEYES  table and puts both hands down, leaning on it.*)
Just what *have* you been teaching?

KEYES
(*with conviction*)
Science.

SCHURHOLZ
You'll have to do better than that.

KEYES
(*stubbornly*)
*Good* science.

SCHURHOLZ
(*Spotting the stack of books, he picks up the closest one, puts his glasses on, and flips open the cover.*)
This?
    (*He thumbs through the pages randomly, then puts the book down. He takes off his glasses and continues speaking, visibly weary.*)

Such books, Orson. I am almost surprised at you. What happened to the man I knew, hmm? What happened to the scientist? The teacher?

(*He motions to the stack of books dismissively.*)

Creationist propaganda is not science.

(*He turns away.*)

KEYES

(*He stares at the stack of books for a moment, then picks up the book SCHURHOLZ has just dropped. He, too, opens the cover and stares at the words thoughtfully. Then he slowly stands.*)

Professor Schurholz has a way with words. He also seems to be clairvoyant. He has dismissed this entire collection of books as "creationist propaganda" without even reading them.

SCHURHOLZ

I don't have to read them to know what they say.

KEYES

(*He comes out from behind the table.*)

Really? You can tell just by looking at a book what sort of religious ideas its author adheres to?

SCHURHOLZ

In certain contexts, yes.

KEYES

I *have* read this book, and yet I still don't know whether the author is catholic, protestant, or just an old-fashioned agnostic.

SCHURHOLZ

(*He goes back to his raised seat behind the table.*)

My wife was a lousy cook. When she fixed breakfast I didn't have to actually eat it to know that she was going to burn the eggs.

(*There are a few scattered laughs in the crowd. SCHURHOLZ is emboldened. He sits triumphantly.*)

I have read many books by these so-called "creation scientists." Men who confuse faith with science are *predictable*, Orson.

KEYES

So these books are all just the rantings of confused men?

SCHURHOLZ

Confused and ignorant.

KEYES

All of them?

SCHURHOLZ

Undoubtedly.

KEYES
(*He goes over to the stack, finds a different book, and opens the cover. He speaks with his back to the Board, so that they cannot see the book.*)
Take this one, then, Willem. Here's some of the propaganda I've been teaching. What sort of religion do you suppose this book offers?

SCHURHOLZ
(*impatiently*)
As I said, I don't have to read it specifically to know what it says in general.

KEYES

So you couldn't quote something from, say -
(*KEYES flips the book open at random.*)
page ninety six?

SCHURHOLZ

Of course not. (*scoffing*) Why would I want to?

KEYES
(*He approaches the Board's table.*)
Well, you wrote it, for one thing.
(*He turns the book around and sets it on the table.*)
"Prehistoric Life," by Dr. Willem Schurholz.

(*The crowd begins to talk at once. SCHURHOLZ stares at the book, his mouth open. VAUGHN smiles. Even BOOKNIGHT chuckles.*)

CRIPPIN
(*standing*)
Quiet! I - will - have - quiet!

*(As the commotion dies down, CRIPPIN looks back and forth between KEYES and SCHURHOLZ.)*
Professor Keyes, I believe you are trying to discredit this hearing.

KEYES

That's right, I am.

CRIPPIN
*(She is not sure what to say to this.)*
Well ... Stop it.

KEYES

Professor Schurholz has tried to discredit an entire field of scientific research by labeling it "propaganda."

SCHURHOLZ
*(coldly)*
I think, Orson, that taking a man's work out of context is the most dishonest form of propaganda imaginable.

KEYES

I quite agree, Willem. Which is why I resent this hearing.

CRIPPIN
*(forcefully)*
You are here so that we can ascertain certain facts.

KEYES

Such as whether or not I am a creationist?

CRIPPIN

Yes.

KEYES
*(wheeling)*
Now, why is that?

CRIPPIN

As we have said -

KEYES

Are creationists prohibited from teaching science at this university?

CRIPPIN
(*Realizing she has made a mistake, backtracking*)
Well, technically, the answer would depend upon -

KEYES
State and Federal laws are pretty clear about discrimination. Does
Springdale University really determine whether a person is employable
based on their religious beliefs?

SCHURHOLZ
The issue is not whether you personally hold creationism to be true, but
whether you are teaching it in the classroom.

KEYES
But I've already told you. Why would I teach something as profession-
ally unpopular as creationism when I do not hold it to be true?

CRIPPIN
What we are concerned with here is the teaching of acceptable science.

KEYES
"Acceptable" science? Now what does *that* mean?

CRIPPIN
It means science.

KEYES
Science.
(*The words come easily, his teaching skill comes out*)
Meaning: empirically verifiable knowledge. Something we can reason-
ably point to as true because we can measure it or confirm it through
natural means?

CRIPPIN
(*relieved*)
Yes.

SCHURHOLZ
(*emphatically*)
No!

KEYES

No?


SCHURHOLZ

You will not tongue-tie this Board with terminology. Because a thing is not verifiable does not mean that it isn't science.


KEYES

Really? Then on what grounds do you disqualify creationism?


SCHURHOLZ
(*condescendingly*)
You can't hide behind pithy words, Orson.


CRIPPIN
(*She has had enough of the technical wrangling.*)
This university will teach science in the science classroom.


KEYES
(*not angrily*)
All right. We will teach science. But you have not made your position clear. Is it the goal of this hearing to determine whether or not I am a creationist?


CRIPPIN
(*Looking at SCHURHOLZ, then at the crowd, then back at SCHURHOLZ. She is trying to think quickly.*)
No. Your personal beliefs are of no consequence here.


KEYES
(*smiling ironically*)
Good. I'd hate to find out after six years that Springdale University was intolerant.
(*Sitting down*)
It happens that I am *not* a creationist. As I said earlier.


CRIPPIN
(*looking at her watch*)
We all seem to be on edge. I think this is a good time for a break. We will reconvene in twenty minutes.
(*The crowd stands and begins to break up as the students, talking*)

*easily, move off. The room slowly clears. SCHURHOLZ and*
*BOOKNIGHT speak together behind the table, then leave.*
*CRIPPIN gathers the student evaluations into an envelope and*
*carries them off. Standing, VAUGHN hesitates behind the table as*
*the room empties. He starts to go, too, then approaches KEYES*
*warily.)*

VAUGHN

Keyes ... Orson. (*He looks down*) I think I understand what you're trying to do.

KEYES
(*surprised*)

Oh? I'm glad to hear it.

VAUGHN

Must be harder in the sciences. Algebra is pretty structured.

KEYES
(*puzzled*)

I'm not sure I follow you.

VAUGHN

I don't blame, you, that's all.
   (*He reads the confusion on Keyes' face.*)
You know, for denying that you're a creationist.

KEYES

But I'm *not* a creationist.

VAUGHN
(*looking around, speaking privately*)

It's all right. I'm a creationist, too.

KEYES
(*skeptically*)

You are?

VAUGHN

Not much room for it either way in my department. But I like to think
the Truth shines through.

*(TESS enters downstage right, approaches quietly, listening. She carries a folded newspaper.)*

KEYES

But ... you don't say anything?

VAUGHN

How can I? You know the meat-grinder they put you through when they find out you have ... beliefs.

KEYES

You're a Christian?

VAUGHN
*(hesitantly, unsure now of where KEYES stands)*
Well ... yes. Like you.

KEYES

I'm not a Christian. I'm not a creationist, either. I'm just a man who asks questions, that's all. I want the right to make up my own mind. Or even to *not* make up my mind when I'm not sure of something.

VAUGHN
*(confused)*
When you're not sure?

KEYES

I suspect we may have taken a wrong turn somewhere. We've become dogmatic. In our zeal for answers, we've made natural science a religion. And we're no longer willing to admit that we might be wrong.
*(VAUGHN begins to back away, surprised. KEYES continues gently)*
Corey, look. Do you really believe that this stuff -
*(He rubs his fingers together as though he feels the earth slipping through them.)*
called life is the handiwork of God?
*(VAUGHN doesn't answer)*
Then why don't you say so? You have the right. If it's the Truth, what are you afraid of?

VAUGHN

How can you ask me that?


KEYES

Part of me envies you. I wish I could be certain of something so important.


VAUGHN
 (*His eyes shift nervously. He sees TESS, and backs away.*)
I - I apologize if I -
 (*He turns away, looking down*)
Well, good luck, anyway.


 (*VAUGHN exits. KEYES turns, sees TESS, sighs.*)


TESS

You mustn't envy him.


KEYES

No?


TESS

Conviction without courage is private torment. (*darkly*) How did it go?


KEYES

Time to update my resume.


TESS

They're fools. They couldn't possibly find someone qualified to replace
you.


KEYES

They can replace anyone. College professors are the barnacles of higher
education. The problem is how to get rid of them.


TESS

Schurholz?


KEYES

And a stack of student evaluations.

TESS

Tell me about it?

KEYES

(*He goes to the table, begins to go through his books, checking the titles, putting them in order in neat stacks. Now, for the first time, he looks worried.*)

I'm a bible thumper. A religious nut. I force my doctrine down the throats of my students.

TESS

(*looking away*)

That bad?

KEYES

(*sarcastically*)

Did you know that Adam and Eve rode dinosaurs? Or that the Earth was only six thousand years old?

TESS

(*Slowly she holds out the newspaper for him to see.*)

Actually, I did.

KEYES

(*He looks at it for a moment, as though it were something distasteful, then reaches out and takes it. He reads, scanning quickly, then folds it back up and sets it down on the desk, gently.*)

If I knew one way or another ... (*shaking his head*) It just ... it seems kind of silly to get martyred for something you don't even believe in.

TESS

(*with conviction*)

Whatever they say about you, whatever they print, you're standing for the truth. That's why they mock you.

(*He is surprised at her. He reaches out to take her arm. TESS covers her mouth with her hand, fighting back her emotions.*)

KEYES

I thought you didn't believe in the truth.

TESS
(*movingly*)
I don't know! I don't know what's right. But I do know what's wrong.
And it's wrong for them to make up a bunch of lies about a man because
they don't like what he says.

KEYES
When Willem read the evaluations out loud, I thought, I don't know.
What's it all for? My students haven't listened to me. Not really. Not
if they heard what they wrote on those forms. Maybe I should just quit.
Go somewhere else to teach.

TESS
They don't want you to quit, Orson. They want you to give in. So they
can say that you've seen the light. That you've changed, and everything
you've said has been a lie.

KEYES
(*He goes back to straightening his books.*)
They know I won't do that.

TESS
Really? Everyone else gives in to them. Why should they expect you to
be any different?

KEYES
(*He frowns, pausing in his actions for just a moment, then
continues.*)
I won't believe that Willem could stoop to arm-twisting.

TESS
Then you're naive, Orson.
(*He looks up at her. They stand there staring at each other,
KEYES surprised at her anger, TESS seething with frustration.*)
Why do you still expect anything good from other people?

KEYES
(*after a pause*)
Because I don't want to be like them.

TESS
Well, congratulations. You're not.

KEYES
(*He holds one book in his hand, weighing it against his palm.*)
So.  What do you think I should do?

TESS
I don't know.

KEYES
Okay, what do you *feel* I should do?

TESS
I *think* ...
(*The words come with unbearable difficulty.  She does not want to say them.*)

KEYES
(*reaching out his hand to her, as though to hold her up*)
Yes?

TESS
(*She takes his hand briefly -*)
I think ... that you should fight it.  Fight it with everything you have.

KEYES
Regardless of what happens?
(*- and then she lets go.*)

TESS
Oh, Orson.  You already know what's going to happen.

*The lights fade*


Scene 2

*Later in the day.  The Hearing is under full swing.  Spectators are packed into the gallery.  KEYES has rolled up his shirt sleeves; he seems more comfortable now.  TESS sits calmly behind him, her hands in her lap.*

*BOOKNIGHT is sitting on the edge of the Board table, facing KEYES.*

                        BOOKNIGHT
And yet you deny that you are a Creationist.

                          KEYES
Yes.

                        BOOKNIGHT
But not that you have beliefs.

                          KEYES
Everyone has beliefs.

                        BOOKNIGHT
Everyone is not a scientist.  You *are* a scientist, aren't you?

                          KEYES
Meaning what?  That scientists can't have personal beliefs about God?
(*to CRIPPIN*) You said my beliefs weren't in question here.

                        BOOKNIGHT
I don't think anyone intends to hold your religious bent against you personally.

                          KEYES
                        (*offended*)
Religious *bent*?

                        BOOKNIGHT
However - and I say this as an outsider looking in - your duties as a sci-
entist depend greatly on the assumptions you make about the universe.
Don't you agree?

                          KEYES
                        (*tiredly*)
My duties as a scientist require that I avoid making assumptions at all.

                        BOOKNIGHT
                       (*smilingly*)
I'm not sure that Dr. Schurholz would agree with you.

SCHURHOLZ
(*with great confidence*)
One cannot draw unbiased conclusions regarding natural causes if one
entertains the possibility of the supernatural.

BOOKNIGHT
In other words, you can't be a scientist and still believe in God. (*to
SCHURHOLZ*) Correct?

SCHURHOLZ
Correct.

BOOKNIGHT
Which is why people of my persuasion (*smoothly, to KEYES*) - *our* persuasion - ought to confine our intellectual pursuits to the realm of the
spirit. Where they belong.

KEYES
Throw out certain possibilities because we don't like where they lead us?

SCHURHOLZ
Belief in God is not scientific, Orson.

KEYES
Atheism is not scientific, either. What happened to letting the evidence
guide our conclusions?

SCHURHOLZ
We *have* evidence.

KEYES
Then what are we afraid of?

SCHURHOLZ
I am afraid of religious zealots who pervert sound scientific principles,
and then teach others to do the same.

KEYES
(*incredulously*)
You won't allow even the possibility of God in the universe? (*to
BOOKNIGHT*) What have they done to you, David? What are you
afraid of losing?

BOOKNIGHT
(*coolly*)
Dr. Keyes, what could I - of all people - possibly stand to lose by admitting God into the Natural world?

KEYES
Your job, apparently.

BOOKNIGHT
(*condescendingly*)
Let me assure you I'm not about to lose my job over God.

KEYES
Your status as a professor at one of the top universities in the nation. Your corner market peddling ambiguous answers to the great puzzle of life. Don't tell me you haven't heard yourself teach, David. Mysteries debunked, two for one!? Truth twisted for next to nothing!?

BOOKNIGHT
(*smiling arrogantly*)
I hold a doctorate of divinity!

KEYES
You hold a piece of paper. They let you spout platitudes and translate Greek manuscripts because you've agreed to stay behind the fence they've put up around you.

BOOKNIGHT
It is *your* doctrine that is being questioned here, not mine.

KEYES
Good for you. Stick to your generalities, Doctor. Keep talking about the "realm of the spirit" They love that. They'll pat you on the back for it.

BOOKNIGHT
You really are arrogant, aren't you?

KEYES
Just don't ever tell them that you think there may be a divine hand shaping the natural world. You'll answer to a God-damned Board of Inquiry!

CRIPPIN

Dr. Keyes, you will not use profanity in this hearing!


KEYES

Profanity?


CRIPPIN

Yes. You said - "God-damned."


KEYES

How can that be profanity if God doesn't exist?


CRIPPIN
(pontificating)

Orson, you know very well that social conventions -- constitute the very -- the very skeleton of productive communication and - and form a basis around which congenial discourse can be built towards a view of - of - of cooperative progress.

(They all stare at her.)


KEYES

In other words, it just is.


CRIPPIN
(with dignity - after a pause)

Yes.


KEYES
(to CRIPPIN, exasperated)

Look, the only assumption a scientist ought to make about the origin of the universe is that God may or may *not* exist.


SCHURHOLZ
(calmly)

Orson, you worry me. You know that supernatural events like the creation of the world by an Almighty God lie outside the purview of science.


KEYES

But it isn't rational to say that supernatural events can't happen just because we can't measure them.

BOOKNIGHT
(*shaking his head*)
But Dr. Schurholz did not say that supernatural events can't happen.
Just that they aren't science.


KEYES
On the contrary, he won't even admit what science is. I say - for starters
- that science is empirically verifiable knowledge. He says that science
is -
(*gesturing in frustration*)
... whatever the hell he says it is.


CRIPPIN
Professor Keyes, I *asked* you not to use profanity.


SCHURHOLZ
Goddammit, Orson, you know very well what science is!


KEYES
Until today, I thought I did.


SCHURHOLZ
(*emphatically*)
All right. I'll spell it out for you. Science is reality.


KEYES
(*appalled*)
Reality?


SCHURHOLZ
Yes.


KEYES
So unscientific things aren't real?!
(*There is a pause as they consider this statement.*)
What about history? Philosophy? Art? None of these things are scien-
tifically measurable. Does this mean they aren't real?


SCHURHOLZ
You are twisting my words.

KEYES

No, I am *un*twisting them.

(*He stands.*)

Science is not mysterious. It is not some secret club for a few privileged intellectuals. For people with Ph.D's and publishing credentials.

(*He turns, sees the students in the gallery, and begins to speak to them. His tone grows suddenly more confident as he sees their faces.*)

Science is not reality. It's a way of trying to *understand* reality. It's a way of knowing about things by looking at them, measuring them, putting them in a beaker and seeing what happens when you add hydrochloric acid.

(*He puts his hand on the stack of books as though for strength.*)

Doctor Schurholz disagrees with me about this. He thinks that some ideas are scientific - and therefore real - even if we can't see them, can't measure them, can't tell our students how they work.

(*He turns back and looks at BOOKNIGHT*)

You know why he says that, David?

BOOKNIGHT

I believe I do.

SCHURHOLZ

(*icily - the words are measured*)

Why don't you tell us, Orson?

KEYES

(*He takes off his tie slowly, places it on the table next to the books, and comes out from around the table.*)

Because Professor Schurholz knows that the theory of evolution - as we currently understand it - is not observable, not measurable, not repeatable. In that regard, Darwin's theory isn't really any more scientific than the Biblical flood!

(*At this there is a collective gasp, followed by a moment of silence, and suddenly the STUDENTS in the gallery begin to talk at once. A few take this opportunity to hurl insults.*)

STUDENT #3

Bible-thumper!

STUDENT #5
Idiot!


STUDENT #6
Jesus Freak!


CRIPPIN
Quiet please! Quiet!


SCHURHOLZ
Now we begin to see.


KEYES
You wanted to know what I've been teaching them in the classroom?


SCHURHOLZ
I believe we know already.


CRIPPIN
(*to the gallery*)
Quiet!


KEYES
(*waiting for the gallery to quiet*)
But you don't know. I merely told them that we don't have a mecha-nism.


SCHURHOLZ
(*thunderously*)
You what!?!


KEYES
(*calmly*)
I told them we don't have a mechanism for change.


SCHURHOLZ
(*For the first time, Schurholz is virtually speechless.*)
You - You - told them -
   (*Dumbfounded - To CRIPPIN:*)
Must we hear any more of this?

KEYES

*(KEYES plays to the gallery again. He realizes suddenly that this*
*- the battle for the students - is the battle he must win.)*
The best idea we have about how evolution works is that every once in
a while, a creature is born genetically different from its parents. They're
called mutations, and most of them don't survive because they have too
many problems. But a few of them - say, one out of a million - are better off than their parents were. Natural Selection then ensures that this
new organism thrives.

The problem is, we've never seen this happen. We can't watch it happen, we can't measure it, we don't really even know if it *could* happen
this way because so much depends on random processes creating complex information.

SCHURHOLZ

*(finding his voice at last)*
We know very well!

KEYES

*(more slowly)*
We think we know. We tell ourselves we know. But we don't really.
We don't know how the loss of information that seems to happen in a
mutation can make something go from simple to complex.

SCHURHOLZ

Loss of information?

KEYES

What else can you call it, Willem? No matter how many fruit flies we
alter, the change always seems to result in a genetic loss.

BOOKNIGHT

Really, Orson! I know for a fact that Willem's students have produced
fruit flies with an extra set of wings.

KEYES

*(easily - BOOKNIGHT is on his territory now.)*
Yes. I know that research.

BOOKNIGHT
(*condescendingly, as though he has caught KEYES in a lie*)
And yet you say that mutations *always* result in a loss of information?


KEYES
I said they always *seem* to.


BOOKNIGHT
But surely that is a contradiction! Professor Schurholz's little flies are blessed with an extra set of wings! Clearly that is new information!


KEYES
No. It is a copying error. And it is hardly beneficial. Those particular flies can't fly. They don't have any muscles attached to their wings.


BOOKNIGHT
(*Looking to SCHURHOLZ in surprise. He did not know this.*)
Is that true?


SCHURHOLZ
It proves nothing, David. Except that a once-great teacher has surrendered his intellect to the disease of faith.


BOOKNIGHT
(*gently*)
Well - I wouldn't call faith a *disease*, Willem.


KEYES
*Faith*? You're the one asking these kids to accept something no one has ever seen.


SCHURHOLZ
But we *have* seen evolution happen!


KEYES
We have?


SCHURHOLZ
You yourself wrote a term paper about the peppered moths of the industrial revolution. I remember it very well.

KEYES

Ah, yes. The peppered moths.

BOOKNIGHT
(*shaking his head*)
I think I am not alone when I say that I find myself at a loss here.

KEYES

Knock yourself out, Willem.

SCHURHOLZ
(*comfortably*)
During the Industrial Revolution the peppered moth of central England changed very quickly as a result of its environment. Originally, these moths were mottled white and brown. But as soot from nearby factories began to cover the trees, they evolved a darker camouflage to help them hide from the birds. When the factories were cleaned up, the moths got back their original colors. So you see? We *have* observed evolution. It's going on around us all the time, if we'd just open our eyes.

KEYES

That's a nice story, but you haven't told the rest of it.

VAUGHN

What do you mean, Orson?

KEYES

Our Biology text shows pictures of light and dark peppered moths resting on a tree. It doesn't mention that the moths in the photo are dead. That they'd been glued to the tree because live peppered moths don't land on tree bark. Nor does the text mention the flaws in the original data -

SCHURHOLZ
(*challenging him*)
What about the panda's thumb, Orson?

KEYES

The panda doesn't *have* a thumb, Willem. It has a spur.

SCHURHOLZ

Exactly! A failed attempt! Nature's mistake! An excellent example of where evolution took a wrong turn.

(*approaching KEYES eagerly*)

If God really exists, Orson, why would He - or She - design the panda's thumb so poorly that it cannot be used for anything but to strip bamboo?

(*He waits confidently*)

KEYES

If God exists, Willem, I haven't the foggiest idea why He, She, or It does anything. The panda's spur isn't *trying* to be a thumb. It's a spur, that's all. And it functions quite well for stripping bamboo.

SCHURHOLZ

(*staring at KEYES oddly, as though trying to understand him.*)

You have a very strange way of interpreting facts.

KEYES

I was thinking the same thing about you.

SCHURHOLZ

Are you not willing, then, to consider the fossil evidence?

KEYES

(*exasperated*)

I'm willing to consider *any* evidence.

SCHURHOLZ

Then why do you deny the fossil record?

KEYES

I *don't* deny the fossil record. I deny your interpretation of it. I deny your pre-packaged stories about what it means. You want to wrap up earth's history in a neat little box.

SCHURHOLZ

I want evidence.

KEYES

What you want is for evolution to be true.

SCHURHOLZ
(*pounding the table with an open palm*)
Evolution *is* true! It's a fact! The fossil record is a fact! Science is a fact!

KEYES
You're being dogmatic.

SCHURHOLZ
And you're being evasive. You won't discuss the fossil record!

KEYES
I'll discuss it all you like. Shall we start with the Cambrian explosion?

SCHURHOLZ
The fossil record is crystal clear, Orson. Absolute evidence of species changing over time. Older, simpler forms giving way to more complex organisms through the eons.

KEYES
Thousands upon thousand of species in the rocks. And not one clearly transitional form. Now why is that?

SCHURHOLZ
You know that we haven't had the time -

KEYES
We've recorded millions of fossils, Willem. Where are the transitions Darwin predicted? They're not in the fossil record.

SCHURHOLZ
(*angrily*)
Just because the record is imperfect does not mean that we can't learn from it.

KEYES
But learn *what*? When we find something we like in the fossil record, we call it proof. When we don't, we say it's a problem with the rocks.

SCHURHOLZ
I'm sorry for you, Orson. I suppose you've told your students that life began because God said, "Let there be."

*(The students in the gallery have gone quiet now. They are not sure whom to believe.)*

KEYES

No, I told them that science hasn't given us the faintest clue about the origin of life.

SCHURHOLZ

Then you are no longer fit to be called a teacher.

VAUGHN

Dean Crippin, I object to that comment. Professor Schurholz is drawing conclusions and the hearing is far from over.

BOOKNIGHT

He was not casting a vote, Corey. Merely expressing an opinion.

CRIPPIN
*(grudgingly)*

The point is acknowledged.

KEYES

I'm not fit to teach? Because I will not tell my students that something no one has ever seen must be accepted blindly as scientific fact? Or else they are not rational? What is the difference between what you want me to force-feed them and some blind religious faith?

SCHURHOLZ
*(ignoring CRIPPIN's remark to him. His voice begins to take on a fanatical and dictatorial tone.)*

You are not fit to teach because you are not teaching science. You are teaching myth. Life originated in a primordial soup as a result of the chance combination of atoms into amino acids and proteins.

KEYES

Because I won't tell them that successive losses of information can make something go from simple to complex?

SCHURHOLZ
*(beginning to rant)*

The Miller-Urey experiment clearly demonstrated that lightning could have released the energy necessary to produce all the ingredients of the first living organism!

KEYES

Because I won't tell them that - (*searching for the right allegory*) - that if they rip enough pages out of an Agatha Christy novel they will eventually find themselves holding a copy of *War and Peace*?

SCHURHOLZ
(*ignoring KEYES - now he, too, plays to the gallery, as though sensing that they are slipping away from him.*)
And once this happened, the chance recombinations of peptide bonds in the first primitive DNA enabled Natural Selection to make a great diversity of living organisms from a single common ancestor, which is something no real scientist disputes.

KEYES

Life is a result of random processes?  Without question?

SCHURHOLZ
(*continuing his speech*)
Random processes, yes, that fashioned the plants, the fish, the reptiles, the insects, the mammals, the crustaceans -

KEYES

Purposeless forces ... Mindless and impersonal?

SCHURHOLZ
(*with the quiet fervor of a visionary*)
Yes, yes, yes!  The inexorable and unfeeling power of evolutionary forces unleashed by the creativity of random processes!

KEYES

Chance - by itself - produces complex information?

SCHURHOLZ
(*softly now, almost kindly*)
You *know* it does, Orson.  Over vast amounts of time, the laws of chance dictate that anything is possible.  Anything and everything.  Even life.  Even human life.

KEYES

Even God?


SCHURHOLZ

(*He stares at KEYES for a moment as though with sudden revelation. When he speaks again, he takes great pains to speak gently and with genuine pity. He seems to understand now that Orson is suffering from the delusions of a temporary fever.*)
What's wrong with you, Orson? You were such a good student. Now you bring up God?


KEYES

You said anything was possible. I just wondered if you meant it.


TESS

Orson.


SCHURHOLZ
(*softly, appealing to her*)
Do you hear this, Dean Crippin? Will you continue to let this man poison the minds of these students with his ... religious nonsense? I request that we dismiss this hearing and reconvene in a closed setting.

(*The STUDENTS in the gallery greet this suggestion with murmurs of disapproval. Schurholz has lost the momentum of their sympathy, and this fact surprises him.*)


TESS
(*more distraught now*)
Orson, please!


KEYES
(*to SCHURHOLZ*)
Poison their minds? With the truth?


BOOKNIGHT
(*to KEYES*)
You seem to think that the Truth is whatever comes out of your own mouth.

VAUGHN
(*seeing his chance*)
Surely these students are mature enough to weigh these arguments for themselves.

SCHURHOLZ
But we do not *want* them weighing these arguments for themselves!
  (*This is greeted with a mixture of boos and hisses. Their displeasure astonishes SCHURHOLZ.*)
It is - it is simply not necessary to cloud the issue with unscientific rhetoric. (*to CRIPPIN*) Dean Crippin, if we do not stop this now, who knows what these young people will end up believing?

CRIPPIN
David, Willem, Corey. (*Motioning to them*) May I speak with you privately?

  (*SCHURHOLZ, BOOKNIGHT, and VAUGHN huddle around CRIPPIN as she speaks to them. Their conversation is apparently heated, though no one else can hear what they are saying.*)

TESS
(*insistently*)
Orson!

KEYES
What is it, Tess?

  (*He faces her, looking the direction of the students. She is facing towards the Board.*)

TESS
You have to stop. Now. Before it's too late.

KEYES
Stop?

TESS
It isn't worth it. You aren't winning anything.
  (*She looks at the Board with fear.*)
You aren't changing their minds. Can't you see that?

KEYES
(*But KEYES is not facing the Board. He is looking at the students in the gallery behind them.*)
No. I don't see that at all. I think they *are* listening. Some of them, anyway.

TESS
(*Still looking at the Board*)
They aren't. You have to try something different. Give them something.

KEYES
(*Surprised*)
What do you think they want?

(*She begins to wring her hands, and after a moment of silence simply looks down without answering.*)

(*At last the private meeting of the Board breaks up. VAUGHN returns to his seat sullenly. SCHURHOLZ scans the crowd with relief.*)

CRIPPIN
(*To the STUDENTS*)
As a result of the - (*looking for the right word*) - of the *mature* content matter of this hearing, we have decided to conduct the final phase in private.

(*Jeers. The STUDENTS begin to protest.*)

STUDENT #5
Who are you trying to protect?

STUDENT #6
What is this, Kindergarten?

STUDENT #3
Keep it open! Open!

(*Dean CRIPPIN holds up her hands for silence, but it is several moments before the room is quiet.*)

CRIPPIN
(*dismissing them*)
Thank you for coming.  Please exit calmly and try not to disrupt the offices on the second floor.

(*The STUDENTS grudgingly make their way out, grumbling as they go.  RODNEY doesn't move as the other students shuffle out.*)

CRIPPIN
(*to RODNEY*)
Young man?

RODNEY
(*with mock surprise*)
You don't mean the press, too?

CRIPPIN
I *especially* mean the press.  You are dismissed.

RODNEY
"Dismissed" huh?

(*RODNEY stands and retreats to the door, pen and paper in hand as he jots down some final notes.  He glances up at the Board, and, finally, at KEYES.*)

RODNEY
(*smiling ironically at KEYES*)
Well, good luck, pal.  You're gonna need it.
(*RODNEY exits*)

CRIPPIN
(*with relief*)
Professor Schurholz, you may continue.

SCHURHOLZ
(*He seems to be out of ammunition now.  He looks from face to face as though he does not know whether his side is winning or losing.  He speaks from insecurity, wanting to be affirmed.*)
I suppose I made my point clearly enough?

BOOKNIGHT

You did.


CRIPPIN

Yes, you were very cogent. I think your explanation will really help these students sort through all this confusion. Well done.


BOOKNIGHT

I couldn't agree more. Why don't you sit down? You were excellent.


KEYES
(*dryly*)

Magnificent, Willem. - Almost evangelical.


CRIPPIN

Really, Orson.


BOOKNIGHT
(*Helping SCHURHOLZ to his seat. To KEYES:*)

Jealousy doesn't become you.


KEYES
(*Returning to his seat wearily*)

Neither does flattery.


CRIPPIN
(*to KEYES*)

We can adjourn until tomorrow, if necessary.


KEYES

I'd like to finish today.


CRIPPIN

David? Did you have anything else you wanted to say?


BOOKNIGHT
(*Considering*)

Just one more question. (*to KEYES*) You say that you are not a creationist. And yet you imply, as I do, that the universe may have been created by an intelligent being. To be blunt, I find it hard to believe you when you say you don't have a religious axe to grind.

*(There is a moment of silence as BOOKNIGHT waits for KEYES to answer. When KEYES offers no response, BOOKNIGHT looks over at CRIPPIN and SCHURHOLZ. He finally grows impatient.)*

### BOOKNIGHT

Well?

### KEYES

Well, what?

### BOOKNIGHT
*(irritated)*
Are you going to answer my question?

### KEYES
*(calmly)*
You didn't ask me a question. You said you find it hard to believe that I don't have a religious axe to grind.

### BOOKNIGHT
*(He throws up his hands in a forced expression of exasperation.)*
Dean Crippin, I don't know what else to do with this man. He seems to fashion himself a martyr.

*(BOOKNIGHT returns to his seat.)*

### CRIPPIN
*(She wears a shallow expression of being contemplative.)*
Professor Keyes, do you have anything you'd like to say to this Board?

### KEYES
You're not being exactly fair, are you?

### CRIPPIN
*(offended)*
What do you mean?

### KEYES
*(pointing to VAUGHN)*
Aren't you going to let *him* have a crack at me?

CRIPPIN
(*glancing from VAUGHN to KEYES*)
He ... I didn't ... Professor Vaughn, did you have anything further to add
to this hearing?

VAUGHN
(*Standing slowly*)
I ...
(*He stares at KEYES for a long moment as the internal battle for
his soul is fought ... and lost.*)
I don't have anything to say.

(*CRIPPIN, BOOKNIGHT, and SCHURHOLZ all smile thinly.
KEYES looks away. VAUGHN sits, stares blankly at the table top
in front of him.*)

CRIPPIN
In that case I will ask you again. Do you have anything you'd like to
say in conclusion?

KEYES
Actually, I do.

CRIPPIN
(*Looking at her watch*)
Well. I hope you will keep it short.

(*As KEYES speaks, STUDENTS begin to emerge on the campus
lawn. They are in a raucous mood, clearly unhappy about being
evicted from the hearing.*)

KEYES
(*He pauses to select a book from his stack*)
A hundred years ago we were arguing about whether or not evolution should be taught in school. The religious folks wanted it kept out
because it didn't fit with their perception of the universe. But they never
wanted to examine whether or not it was true.

STUDENT #3
Whaddaya think, Parker? Freedom of speech?

STUDENT #6
Freedom of assembly.


STUDENT #5
Freedom of information.  They passed an act.

STUDENT #3
They're violating our rights.

STUDENT #6
My folks paid good money for me to go to this school.

STUDENT #5
(*yelling*)
Open the hearing!

KEYES
(*oblivious to the STUDENTS outside*)
Now we've come full circle.  We're still arguing about what to teach in
school.  But now it's us - the scientists - who refuse to ask whether evolution is true.  Somehow, the point has been decided.

STUDENT #3
Yeah!  Open the hearing!

STUDENT #6
Open it!  Open it! Open it!

STUDENT #5
Open it! Open it!


(*Now the phrase becomes another protest mantra*)

STUDENTS
(*together*)
OPEN IT! ... OPEN IT! ... OPEN IT! ... OPEN IT!

BOOKNIGHT
(*Hearing the noise at last, he looks behind him, through the
window.*)

My God, what's going on out there?

CRIPPIN

What do you mean?

SCHURHOLZ

What are they doing?

(*They all crowd to the window, KEYES last.*)

VAUGHN

Good Lord!

(*The STUDENTS have assembled around the gazebo and are rocking it back and forth. They are close to a riot.*)

STUDENTS

OPEN IT! ... OPEN IT! ... OPEN IT!

CRIPPIN

My God! They'll start a riot. They'll demolish the campus. Have they gone crazy?

SCHURHOLZ
(*pointing a finger at KEYES*)

This is *your* fault, Orson.

KEYES
(*shocked*)

*My* fault?

SCHURHOLZ
(*railing*)

*This* is what happens when you confuse them. Tell them absurd stories about God and creation. These kids have to have direction. Not ... options.

KEYES
(*He places the book he has been holding back onto the pile.*)

I'm surprised at you, Willem. I thought you believed that random processes increase order? Well, take a good look, learned colleagues. You want the creative power of chaos?

(*He points out the window.*)

There it is.  You can have it if you want.  But I don't think it will bring you anything good.

(*The STUDENTS' shouting grows louder as the gazebo rocks back and forth, back and forth.*)

STUDENTS

OPEN IT! ... OPEN IT! ... OPEN IT! ... OPEN IT!

*The curtain falls.*

# ACT 3 THREE

ACT III

Scene 1


*Twilight, that same evening.  Dusk is settling over the empty campus, the buildings of which now burn with the soft fire of sunset.*
*SCHURHOLZ and CRIPPIN are alone in the conference room, which, like the rest of the stage, is half-lit with an eerie red glow.*
*SCHURHOLZ stands with his back to the audience, staring through the window to the lawn.  His hands are folded behind his back.*
*CRIPPIN is seated.  They are absorbed in their thoughts--they may have been motionless that way for some time.*


SCHURHOLZ
We don't have a choice now, do we?

CRIPPIN
(*sighing*)
I don't see one.  We haven't had a choice since *The SpringDaily* broke this story.

SCHURHOLZ
I wish there could have been some other way.  I had hoped that reading those evaluations would force him back to us.

CRIPPIN
You did force him out into the open.

SCHURHOLZ
(*with disbelief*)
I threw him softballs!  I invited him to deny any vestige of reliance on God.

CRIPPIN
You called him a creationist.

SCHURHOLZ

I thought he would change his mind if we confronted him with alternatives.

CRIPPIN

No, you didn't.

SCHURHOLZ

(*He turns to look at her, momentarily surprised. Then he turns back to the window.*)
I hoped.

CRIPPIN

At least we found him out. Having a man like that on staff is academic cancer.

SCHURHOLZ

He showed such promise.

CRIPPIN

He chose to fight a losing battle. Plenty of qualified candidates waiting to take his job.
(*She holds up a stack of papers*)
I'm already getting resumes.

SCHURHOLZ

(*Still looking out the window.*)
The campus looks like a demilitarized zone. They would have destroyed the entire university if you hadn't called the campus police. Good thinking, by the way.

CRIPPIN

Too bad we couldn't have put Keyes away quietly. God knows other universities do this sort of thing all the time. And no one says boo.

SCHURHOLZ

That used to be true. But not any more.

CRIPPIN

No?

SCHURHOLZ

The tide is turning against us.

CRIPPIN

Really, Willem. You're being dramatic. This became an issue because we are cursed with the cream of America's crop. We have journalism students who dig for stories - the way we teach them to. At most universities this sort of problem might have festered for years before becoming an issue.

SCHURHOLZ

It's already an issue at most universities. Did you see the stack of books Keyes brought?

CRIPPIN
(*dismissively*)

Props. To make himself look good. To give him strength. He had *your* books in that collection, too, Willem.

SCHURHOLZ

Yes. Mine and many others. He may have been alone at the hearing, but he's not alone. And that's the thought that keeps me awake at night.

CRIPPIN

Along with the thought that he was *your* student?

SCHURHOLZ

He had a great mind.

CRIPPIN

Don't take it so hard.

SCHURHOLZ
(*wistfully*)

Did I ever tell you about his snake?

CRIPPIN
(*Resignedly - she does not really want to hear the story.*)
No.

SCHURHOLZ

It was a copperhead, four feet long. He caught it wild when he was
doing field work for his thesis. Kept it for almost a year. Thought it
would help him pick up girls, I guess. Anyway, one weekend he decided
that it deserved more than a plywood box and a 60-watt bulb.

So, I'll be damned if he didn't drive all the way back to Missouri to
that same God-forsaken field where he found it. And you know what?
It bit him on the ankle when he let it out. He had to be admitted to a
hospital for anti-venom treatments.

CRIPPIN
(*dismayed*)
Good Lord, Willem. You sound as though you're still fond of him!

SCHURHOLZ
(*shrugging*)
I can relate to him, that's all.
(*He returns to the window and gazes out.*)
Now that he's bitten my ankle.

CRIPPIN

This will all be over soon.

SCHURHOLZ
(*gloomily - still staring out*)
There are others out there. Others just like him.

CRIPPIN
(*knowingly*)
Not as many as you think.

SCHURHOLZ

Oh? This whole inquiry was based on just four evaluations. Four!
(*shaking his head*)
Out of all the students who took his classes - all those years - only four
saw where Keyes was headed. You think there aren't many religious
nuts out there?
(*distastefully*)
I think there are more of them every day. They're like rabbits.

CRIPPIN

*Frightened* rabbits. In the end, most of them don't have the courage to stand up for what they believe. Not here. Not where it counts.

(*BOOKNIGHT enters, followed by VAUGHN*)

BOOKNIGHT
(*cheerfully*)

You didn't start the funeral without us?

CRIPPIN

No. We all have to be here to vote.

BOOKNIGHT

Sorry for the delay. We were detained.

VAUGHN

Someone wants to speak to us.

BOOKNIGHT

That is, collectively. (*to Crippin*) Do you mind?

(*CRIPPIN looks to SCHURHOLZ, who shrugs passively*)

CRIPPIN

All right.

BOOKNIGHT
(*to VAUGHN*)

Corey?

(*BOOKNIGHT and SCHURHOLZ take their seats behind the table.*)

VAUGHN

I'll get her.

(*VAUGHN opens the door, sticks his head in the hallway, and motions to the person who is waiting there. Then he also sits.*)

(*TESS DeSilva enters, pauses in the doorway. She clutches her purse in both hands.*)

TESS
(*with professional dignity*)
Dean Crippin.  Willem.


SCHURHOLZ
Tess.


CRIPPIN
(*coldly*)
Professor DeSilva.  How can we help you?


TESS
Have you made a decision yet?  About Orson?


CRIPPIN
(*flatly*)
I'm afraid that information is confidential.


TESS
You haven't decided yet, have you?  One way or the other. You haven't
voted yet?


SCHURHOLZ
No.
   (*CRIPPIN looks at SCHURHOLZ sternly, but he ignores her*)
We haven't voted yet.


TESS
I thought maybe ...


BOOKNIGHT
(*kindly*)
It's all right.  Just tell us what you came to say.


(*TESS's professional demeanor begins to collapse as she speaks.
This is unbearably difficult for her.*)


TESS
You're going to fire him, aren't you?  Oh, I know you haven't voted yet.
But I could tell during the hearing that it didn't go well for him.
   (*They stare in silence.  This makes her more agitated.  She begins
   to wring her hands.*)

He didn't - he didn't make his case well, did he?  And now you don't have a choice, because of what the paper is printing.  About him being a creationist.  But you know he isn't.

(*Her voice rises - she sounds almost frantic.*)

You know he *isn't* a creationist.  He isn't all those things that the paper is printing, and you know it.

CRIPPIN

Professor DeSilva -

TESS

He just isn't, and you know it!

SCHURHOLZ
(*gently - with genuine sympathy*)

Tess.

(*SCHURHOLZ's voice seems to soothe her a little.  She looks down, as though ashamed.*)

We all know it isn't your fault.

TESS

But -

SCHURHOLZ

We all know there was nothing you could do.

BOOKNIGHT
(*oozing pity*)

You can't help it if you love him.

CRIPPIN
(*with a trace of warmth now*)

You'll have to leave this to us, now, Tess.  It is out of your hands.

TESS

Because you don't have a choice, right?

BOOKNIGHT
(*sympathetically*)

That's right, sweetheart.  We don't have a choice.

TESS
(*brightening*)
But - but I could give you one!


CRIPPIN
(*forcefully*)
Really, dear, it would be better for you to leave now and let us handle this situation.


TESS
(*angrily - they are all shocked by the force of her response.*)
Don't call me dear!
(*They stare at her in silence and she looks down.*)
But I could! I could give you a choice.
(*She reaches into her purse.*)
I wondered why all of you didn't think of it. It seems so obvious.
(*She withdraws a folded piece of paper, and unfolds it carefully.
She begins to ramble as she speaks - hope brings too many
words for her to arrange carefully.*)
It was all the media attention that got him into this mess. What the
paper printed. What people think. Made everyone have to take sides,
either or. When taking sides is the last thing Orson wants. So I thought
perhaps a little clarity ...
(*She comes forward, the paper held out to each of them in turn:
CRIPPIN, BOOKNIGHT, SCHURHOLZ. They will not take it. At
last she offers it to VAUGHN, who accepts it with a reluctant
smile.*)
The media got us into this. Maybe they can get us out.


(*VAUGHN has been reading the slip of paper as she speaks, but he
is no longer smiling. He sets it down on the table with obvious
distaste.*)


VAUGHN
I don't think this will work.


TESS
But it will! I know it will! You, of all people, should -
(*She stops mid-sentence, her thoughts following a sudden
realization. VAUGHN looks away.*)

SCHURHOLZ
(*He picks up the paper, puts on his glasses, and reads. After a pause:*)
Actually -
(*He hands the paper to BOOKNIGHT, who now reads it, and takes off his glasses. He looks at TESS with surprise.*)
I don't know why it wouldn't. If Orson is willing.

BOOKNIGHT
(*after reading it*)
We'll have to schedule a news conference. (*thinking*) But that shouldn't be a problem.

CRIPPIN
(*impatiently*)
Well? What is it?

(*BOOKNIGHT hands her the paper and she reads it.*)

CRIPPIN
Good Lord.

SCHURHOLZ
You may have hit on the solution, Tess.

TESS
Do you think so?

SCHURHOLZ
Thank you.

CRIPPIN
(*wonderingly*)
But do you think Keyes will do it?

SCHURHOLZ
He might. He just might. They aren't *his* words, after all. He could keep his pride.

BOOKNIGHT
Whatever else he is, he's not a fool. He knows what's coming.

CRIPPIN

It would certainly solve the problem of our academic reputation.


TESS

(*giddily*)

You mean you'll make him the offer?


CRIPPIN

(*sternly*)

That is an issue for the Board to decide.


TESS

But you'll discuss it?  You will, won't you?


BOOKNIGHT

(*Rising - he shows TESS to the door.*)

Thank you, Tess.  You have been most helpful.


TESS

You'll vote on it tonight?


BOOKNIGHT

Tonight, yes.  We shall.  Now why don't you go home and get some rest?


TESS

(*eagerly*)

Will you call me afterwards, Willem?


SCHURHOLZ

I will.


TESS

Thank you - I think ...

(*TESS exits*)


BOOKNIGHT

(*returning to his seat*)

Amazing woman.


CRIPPIN

I have to say: I am shocked.

SCHURHOLZ
(*distantly*)
One can never tell what a woman will do.

VAUGHN
(*almost to himself*)
I don't think Orson will do it.

BOOKNIGHT
Why not?  If he doesn't, he'll lose everything he values.
  (*grandly*)
As the Book of Proverbs says ...
  (*his voice booms with the caricatured conviction of a televangelist.*)
"He that troubleth his own house shall inherit the wind!"

CRIPPIN
Shall we ask him?  That, clearly, is the question.
  (*They all look to her - the moment has arrived.*)
All in favor -
  (*slowly*)
Raise your hand.
  (*CRIPPIN holds up one hand.  She is followed by BOOKNIGHT
  and SCHURHOLZ.  After a moment, they realize that VAUGHN is
  not holding up his hand, and they stare at him in silence for a few
  seconds.*)
Well, Corey?  Is it unanimous?

  (*VAUGHN looks from face to face, then down.  Slowly, he, too,
  raises his hand.*)


*The lights fade*


Scene 2


*The campus lawn.  A podium jammed with microphones has been
placed on the gazebo.  A crowd of STUDENTS has gathered to hear the
Board s decision.  Several of them carry signs that read:*

*Fire Keyes!*
*God is Dead.*
*Let My People Think!*
*Darwin was right*
*Science not Religion*
*Separation of Church and State*
*Keep Religion out of School*

*The media have also come to hear the decision. RODNEY and SCOTT stand idly to one side. Newspaper REPORTERS talk quietly among themselves, unheard. A television CAMERA PERSON untangles wires in preparation to record the announcement. A NEWS ANCHOR arranges his coat, straightens his tie, smoothes his hair.*

ANCHOR

How much time do we have?

CAMERA PERSON

Two minutes.

ANCHOR

They'll be late.

CAMERA PERSON

You want the podium in the background?

ANCHOR

Get the protestors first, then pan back.

CAMERA PERSON
*(Adjusting the camera on one shoulder.)*
Okay, let's see how it looks.

STUDENT #5
*(pointing)*
Hey, we're gonna be on TV!

STUDENT #7
*(to the ANCHOR)*
What station are you guys with?

                            ANCHOR
                            (*stiffly*)
Five.


                          STUDENT #7
Can you get a shot of me?  My mom thinks all I do is study.


                        CAMERA PERSON
Try the sound.


                            ANCHOR
(*Holding his microphone up and striking a practiced pose. To the
CAMERA PERSON*)
This is Larry Baumgartner, live with action five news.


                        CAMERA PERSON
It's off.  The mike.


                            ANCHOR
(*Switching on the microphone, he strikes his pose again*)
This is Larry Baumgartner, five with live news, from the campus of
Springdale University, where -


                        CAMERA PERSON
Good.  But it's "live with five."


                            ANCHOR
What?


                        CAMERA PERSON
Live with five.  You said "five with live."


(*A group of STUDENTS has gathered behind them, away from
the main cluster of demonstrators.  STUDENT #5 jumps up and
down to get in view.*)


                          STUDENT #7
Hey Mom, guess what I'm learning in college!


                          STUDENT #9
The Earth was created in seven days!

STUDENT #3
(*emphatically*)

*Six* days, you moron.

STUDENT #6

Here they come!

ANCHOR
(*practicing*)

Live with Five.  Live with five.  Live with Fiiiiive, this is Larry Baumgartner at Springdale University.  (*He turns his head to look*)  That should be Keyes now!

(*The group gathers toward the gazebo.  The reporters press to the front.*)

CAMERA PERSON

We'll go on my signal.

ANCHOR

Live with five.

CAMERAMAN

On three.

(*Enter KEYES, followed by CRIPPIN, then SCHURHOLZ, BOOKNIGHT, VAUGHN.  KEYES sees the crowd and pauses, then mounts the steps of the gazebo as though he is about to be hanged.  The other four follow somberly.*)

ANCHOR

How's my hair?

CAMERA PERSON

And two ... and one ...
(*He motions for the ANCHOR to begin with one finger.*)

ANCHOR

This is Larry Baumgartner, action five news, live from Springdale University, where Professor Orson Keyes is about to read a prepared statement.

(*Holding his hand up to one ear*)
No, Kate, at this point there has been no word from the administration as to whether or not Keyes will keep his job. But we do anticipate getting an answer to that question at any moment.

CRIPPIN
(*Stepping up to the podium*)
Ladies and gentlemen.

STUDENT #7
(*shouting*)
Fire Keyes!

(*There is a general outburst from the crowd. The CAMERA PERSON sweeps the camera back and forth to take it in. CRIPPIN waits for the voices to subside.*)

CRIPPIN
(*slowly*)
Ladies ... and gentlemen. The Board of Inquiry has reached a decision. At this time I am pleased to allow Professor Orson Keyes the honor of explaining it.

(*She steps back to make room for KEYES. He hesitates, then goes to the podium.*)

KEYES
There have been a lot of accusations against me lately. As far as I know, the only one that's true is that I teach Biology at Springdale University.
(*This goes over badly.*)
Anyway, the Board decided today that there was not enough evidence to justify letting me go -

(*The STUDENTS break up again, begin to shout and jab their signs into the air. Dean CRIPPIN steps up to the microphone and motions for them to stop.*)

CRIPPIN
Quiet please ... Quiet!

KEYES
But I was told I'd be given a prepared statement.

*(He turns to Crippin, who hands him a folded sheet of paper. He unfolds the paper and sets it on the podium, scans it for the first time, and sighs heavily. He is disappointed. He places the paper on the podium and smoothes it with his palm. The crowd is utterly silent.)*

All I ever wanted was the freedom to evaluate the facts honestly. But there's been so much confusion about my position that I'm supposed to read something to all of you. Just to make everything clear.

*(He hesitates.)*

It's pretty simple really. I can keep my job if I read this sheet of paper to you.

*(He reads it reluctantly.)*

It says, "I hold the theory of evolution, as commonly understood and taught in science courses, to be wholly and completely true. Darwin's theory of evolution is an accurate account of how life arose on our planet and continues to develop today."

*(The crowd is silent. One by one the signs are slowly lowered to the floor.)*

So. Now I've read it.

*(He holds the paper up again, almost as reluctantly as he read it, and begins to carefully tear it into halves as he speaks. He lets the shreds flutter to the floor around him.)*

I've read it, but it isn't honest. I don't know how life got here, and neither does anyone else. Not Professor Schurholz, not Dr. Booknight, not Dean Crippin.

*(The crowd begins to mutter.)*

CRIPPIN

Dr. Keyes -

KEYES

Darwin's theory was brilliant for its time. But modern discoveries in geology, paleontology, and microbiology have brought certain aspects of that theory into doubt. I believe we have the right - and the duty - to keep asking the hard questions until we have concrete answers. Evolution *might* be true. Probably *is* true. But maybe not. We'll never know until we can be honest with ourselves and learn to live with whatever the evidence leads us to. Even...

*(KEYES hesitates as though debating whether to really use these words:)*

...even if that something is God.

*(Now the jeers begin.  Someone in the crowd starts to chant.)*

VOICE
Orson Keyes thinks you're a fool, wants the Bible taught in school!

*(The crowd begins to echo the chant.)*

CROWD
Orson Keyes thinks you're a fool!
  Wants the Bible Taught in School!

*(The crowd quiets just enough to hear CRIPIN's words.)*

CRIPPIN
*(infuriated)*
Doctor Keyes, you are excused!

*(The crowd cheers.)*

*(KEYES is led off the gazebo by VAUGHN as pandemonium
breaks out.  The signs are hoisted skyward again as the
STUDENTS cheer wildly.  KEYES exits, accompanied by
VAUGHN, surrounded by REPORTERS pressing them with
questions.)*

CRIPPIN
*(motioning for quiet)*
The standards of this University will be maintained.  Thank you.

*(CRIPPIN, SCHURHOLZ and BOOKNIGHT exit.  The crowd
breaks up slowly as the STUDENTS exit.)*

ANCHOR
There you have it, Kate.  Dr. Orson Keyes of Springdale University
apparently will *not* have his contract renewed.   This is Larry
Baumgartner, Five with Live.

*(The ANCHOR and CAMERA PERSON exit as reporters Cynthia
TANNER and Luis ESPANOZA approach RODNEY.  RODNEY
has been watching from the fringes as though enjoying a good
show.)*

TANNER

You wouldn't be Rodney Harris?


RODNEY

Who's asking?


TANNER
(*offering her hand*)
Cynthia Tanner, Universal Press.


RODNEY
(*shaking his hand*)
In that case, Rodney Harris, Springdale Daily News.


TANNER

This is my associate, Luis Espanoza.


RODNEY
(*shaking ESPANOZA's hand*)
A pleasure.


TANNER
(*She indicates the thinning crowd with a nod of her head, and
holds up a copy of the newspaper.*)
Was this your work?


RODNEY

I just opened the can.  The worms were already inside.


TANNER
(*She withdraws a business card.*)
My boss is always hunting for fresh talent.  We'll put in a good word for
you.
(*She gives RODNEY the card*)
You wanna see the world?


RODNEY

Are you kidding?  If I don't get out of this back-water mud-puddle soon,
I'll wither up and die.


ESPANOZA

Sound familiar?

TANNER
(*smiling*)
Yeah, I know. Well, there's eight hundred bucks in it for us if you pan out for Universal. Give me a call in a couple of weeks when you graduate.

(*TANNER and ESPANOZA exit. RODNEY sees SCOTT, standing alone apart from the crowd, which has greatly diminished by now. SCOTT is lost in thought.*)

RODNEY
(*He holds up the card triumphantly as he approaches.*)
Scott! Scott! Did you hear that?

SCOTT
(*disturbed - staring at the podium*)
Huh? No.

RODNEY
(*He gives SCOTT the card*)
I told you it would work. I've got a job waiting for me with the U.P. when I graduate.

SCOTT
(*unenthusiastically*)
Oh. That's great.
   (*SCOTT gives the card back.*)

RODNEY
Aren't you going to congratulate me? I've already got a job offer and I'll probably get a dozen more by the end of the week.

SCOTT
Oh. Congratulations.
   (*He turns to look back at the gazebo, the dissipating crowd.*)

RODNEY
(*cheerfully*)
Don't look so glum. Your turn will come next year.

SCOTT
Sure.

RODNEY
(seriously)

You know, I couldn't have done it without you.

*(He holds out his hand in a gesture of thanks. SCOTT shakes his hand without thinking. When he lets go, SCOTT continues to stare at his open palm.)*

What's wrong?

*(SCOTT rubs his hand with the other thumb as though to remove a deep stain, his expression ominous.)*

That will come off. It's just printer's ink.

*(SCOTT looks up at RODNEY as though seeing his face now for the first time. He backs up a step and starts to speak; he is just now realizing something of dreadful importance.)*

Scott?

*(SCOTT's mouth moves awkwardly but no sound comes. At last he turns and exits.)*

I wonder what's wrong with him.

*(RODNEY shrugs and takes a deep breath, realizes that the crowd is now gone and he is all alone. He spies the gazebo, and saunters over to it as though on a whim. He mounts the steps slowly and grips the podium with both hands. The crowd is still there for him, but in the future, rather than the past.)*

*(KEYES enters followed by VAUGHN. RODNEY retreats into the shadows of the gazebo, unseen.)*

VAUGHN

What will you do?

KEYES

I don't know.

VAUGHN

Maybe another school. Some place with more ... tolerance.

KEYES
(knowingly)

After today?

VAUGHN

Perhaps a Christian school?

113

KEYES

No.

(*TESS enters, shell-shocked, her arms folded.  KEYES smiles when he sees her.*)

VAUGHN

I have something I want to say to you.  I ... I'm sorry.

KEYES

I'm sure it wasn't your fault.

VAUGHN

(*He looks away*)
Anyway, I'm sorry.

(*PARKER enters.  He has been looking for KEYES.  He sees Keyes and comes towards him eagerly.*)

KEYES

(*encouragingly - as if to say that he understands, he knows what happened.  To VAUGHN:*)
Maybe someday you'll join me.

(*An expression between horror and joy crosses VAUGHN's face. VAUGHN exits.*)

(*TESS starts to approach KEYES, but Parker inadvertently comes between them first.*)

PARKER

Professor Keyes!

KEYES

(*ironically*)
"Professor?"  Not any more.

PARKER

Todd Parker.  You taught my Freshman biology class last year.

KEYES

I remember you.

PARKER
(*nervously*)
I was wondering about some of those books you mentioned during the hearing.

KEYES
(*surprised*)
You want to borrow something?

PARKER
Do you mind?  I mean, if it's not too much trouble.

KEYES
Not at all.  Come to my office tomorrow morning.  I'll be cleaning out my desk.  You can borrow anything you'd like.

PARKER
(*offering his hand - they shake*)
Thanks.

KEYES
My pleasure.

(*PARKER exits.*)

TESS
(*distantly, with bitter irony*)
Well, *Professor*?

KEYES
(*brightly*)
Tess!

TESS
(*unhappily*)
What happened?

KEYES
Did you just hear that?  Something ... wonderful!

TESS
Wonderful!?

KEYES

Remarkable, really.  Well, of course I lost my job.


TESS
(*bitterly*)

Is that all?


KEYES

And my reputation.


TESS
(*scoffing*)

What reputation?


KEYES

But I found something better.
   (*He points to the saying etched on the Journalism Building.*)
It's true, you know.  The truth really does set you free.


TESS

Free?  From what?


KEYES
(*gently*)

I realized when I was up there behind the podium.  When they gave
me the statement to read.  I don't know why I couldn't see it before.  It
wasn't just Crippin and Schurholz who were trying to control my life.
It was me.  I wanted to be in control of everything, examine everything
under a microscope.  Like in the lab.  A vial for this, a vial for that.


TESS
(*dumbfounded*)

What are you trying to say?


KEYES

I'm sorry, Tess.  I was wrong about us.  I was wrong to put you off.


TESS

I don't understand.

KEYES

I guess I was afraid my emotions would bubble out of their little beaker. But all of a sudden I don't care.

(*He takes her hands in his.*)

Is it too late for me to feel something for you, Tess? I do want to marry you. And whatever I did to mess it up, I'm sorry.

(*tenderly*)

I do love you. With all my heart.


TESS

Oh, Orson -


KEYES

(*He holds her to him, but only for a moment. Then she pushes him away firmly.*)

Tess?


TESS

Don't you understand what you've done?


KEYES

(*happily*)

Yes. I just proposed to you.


TESS

No, no, no! Earlier, you stupid -

(*the words catch in her throat, but she finally forces them out.*)

- you stupid jerk. You threw it all away. Over nothing.


KEYES

(*deflated*)

Tess, I -


TESS

(*furiously*)

Over nothing!


KEYES

It doesn't matter. It's just a job.

TESS

It *does* matter. Orson, why did you do it? Why did you throw your career away over a piece of paper? They gave you a way out. They made it so easy. All you had to do was stop after you read it. You didn't have to mean it. You didn't have to lie. You didn't have to do anything but let it all go.

KEYES

But those words -

TESS

Those words weren't even yours! They were mine!

KEYES
(*shocked*)

Yours?

TESS

Don't you see? You didn't have a way out. They were going to fire you.

KEYES

They did fire me.

TESS

Because you made them.

KEYES

I did everything I could to prevent it.

TESS

You tore up the note.

KEYES

The note was a lie.

TESS

You don't know if it was a lie or not. You said so yourself. You said it might be true. What's the difference?

KEYES

The difference between right and wrong.

TESS

You and your damned absolutes.  Couldn't you compromise just a little?

KEYES
(*hurt*)

You of all people, Tess.

TESS

Why are you looking at me that way?

KEYES

You sound like -

TESS

Like what?
  (*But he will not say it.*)
Like Schurholz?

KEYES

Do you really think that the Truth doesn't matter?

TRESS
(*angrily*)

Truth?  Truth?!!

KEYES

Capital T.

TESS

Did you think this was all just a game?  That some high priced attorney
in a white hat would ride into town and defend you for free?  Did you
think the newspapers would make you a hero?  Put up money to fight
your legal battles?  The days of right and wrong are over.  Truth and
Justice are lies we tell ourselves to make sense of our choices.  What
were you thinking?

KEYES

I was thinking you wanted me to fight them.

TESS

I wanted you to win.

KEYES

I *did* win. I won freedom. I won the right to question. The right to ask, "What if it didn't happen that way?" And I won some of the students, too. Didn't you hear that boy a few minutes ago? They were *listening*, Tess! A few weeks from now, a few years maybe, and the lights will start to come on.

TESS

You *lost*, Orson. Why can't you see that? You lost everything.

KEYES

(*He starts to speak, and then stops as he begins to understand what she is implying. Finally, after a pause, he finds his voice.*)
Everything? Even you?

TESS

I can't do it, Orson, I can't. I can't go with you now. Don't you under-stand? No matter where I go - for the rest of my life I'll be "that cre-ationist's wife." And, dammit, that isn't who you are. It isn't who *I* am. Orson, I can't leave this place. I never wanted to leave Springdale. I wanted you here. And now, the way my friends talk about us. The other teachers. I can't stand to have them look at me with pity me because I love you. I can't bear it.

KEYES

Because you love me?

TESS

Orson -
(*Now she begins to cry. KEYES starts to approach her, stops, then comes closer awkwardly.*)

KEYES
(*numbly*)
It's all right, Tess. It's my fault, not yours. I should have told you what it would cost us. I see that now. All our wonderful, progressive friends. Our Thursday night poetry readings. The aura of Springdale. (*tenderly*) I've never seen you cry before.
(*He lifts her chin in his hand, so she will look at his face. They gaze at each other as though reconciled for a few fleeting moments.*)

TESS

*(She tugs her chin free of his hand and looks away. She will not look at him any longer. She cannot bear to.)*

I'm sorry.

*(TESS turns and exits hurriedly.)*

*(RODNEY, who has been watching from the shadows of the gazebo, now steps out into the light. He claps his hands slowly, as though for a mediocre performance.)*

RODNEY
*(mockingly)*

Bravo, Professor. Well done.

KEYES
*(taken aback)*

What are you doing here?

RODNEY

Catching your latest performance. The argument, the touching good-bye, the boo hoo routine. The whole bit. You know, you're a class act. Got rid of her like yesterday's breakfast.

KEYES

I should have known you'd still be around. In it to the very end.

RODNEY

One thing I can't figure. Where do you go from here? Obviously you got a better offer. One of those Bible schools, maybe?

KEYES

Bible schools?

RODNEY

Don't want to tell me, huh? I guess I don't blame you. Shouldn't be that hard for me to find out, though.

KEYES

Schurholz was right.

RODNEY
(*surprised*)

Oh?


KEYES

You *are* a snake.


RODNEY
(*bowing*)

An *employed* snake, thanks to you.  I guess I have the story close enough, anyway.  You'll escape to Oral Roberts or Bob Jones.  Tess will stay and snuggle up to Schurholz when her bed gets cold.


KEYES

I get it.  Whenever you don't know the answers, you just make them up.


RODNEY

That's how the world works, Professor.


KEYES

Only fools and con-artists believe that.


RODNEY
(*knowingly*)

But the world is made of fools.
   (*He spreads his arms in confession*)
And con-artists.


KEYES

What's so difficult about saying, "I don't know?"


RODNEY

Runs against the grain, against our nature.  You can't get anywhere in life that way.   Even the wrong answer is better than no answer at all.  Look.  I can prove it to you.
   (*He looks around at the lawn, which is now littered with crumpled newspapers, and reaches down to pick one up.*)
Here we are.  (*reading it*)  Professor Genesis.
   (*He gives it to KEYES*)
We'll get one more day out of it.  And I'll get a career.  "Bible-thumper thumped by Board" has a nice ring to it, don't you think?

KEYES
(*unimpressed*)

Clever.


RODNEY
(*grinning*)
You know, you had me going there for a while.  Listening to you, I almost fell for it.  For just a minute, I started to doubt my lack of faith in humanity.  But then I realized.  That stuff about no one really knowing the truth was just a smoke screen.
(*with disdain*)
You can't be for real.


KEYES

Can't be?


RODNEY
All you had to do was say that evolution is an undeniable fact.  Nobody loses everything over nothing.  Nobody.  Not when they can help it.


KEYES
I think you'll make an excellent journalist, Rodney.


RODNEY
(*surprised and flattered*)
Thanks, Professor.  Sure you don't want to tell me where you're going from here?


KEYES

You wouldn't believe me.


RODNEY
(*interested - he thinks Keyes will reveal some new secret.*)
Try me.


KEYES
Promise to quote me in tomorrow's edition?


RODNEY
(*excitedly - he comes closer*)

Absolutely.

KEYES

Word for word?


RODNEY
(*He withdraws paper and a pen from his pocket.*)
Shoot.


KEYES
(*slowly - after a pause*)
I - don't - know.


RODNEY
(*Deflated - he puts the pen and paper back in his pocket without writing anything.*)
And I thought you were finally going to say something profound.


KEYES
(*removing his tie*)
Maybe I did.  Maybe the truth is just too difficult for you to accept.


RODNEY
Not at all.  It's just too boring.


KEYES
(*He starts to put the tie in his pocket, then has a sudden inspiration.*)
Here.
(*He flips the tie to Rodney.*)
For your new job.


RODNEY
(*surprised*)
Your tie?


KEYES
Tess called it a symbol of artificiality.  Personally, I can't stand the things.


RODNEY
(*shrugging*)
You're a piece of work, Professor.
(*RODNEY turns and starts to leave.  He speaks as though to no*

*one, without even turning to look at KEYES.*)
Anything you haven't given up today?


KEYES
(*He looks up, stares at the etching above the door for just a moment, and then says quietly:*)
Yes.


RODNEY
(*Just before exiting, RODNEY seems to remember something. He turns back to Keyes.*)
Oh - I wouldn't hang around here too long. Next time they get their hands on you they're liable to burn you at the stake. And I may just light the match.

(*RODNEY exits*)

(*KEYES watches RODNEY go. He is alone now on campus. He turns in a big circle, taking it in for the last time, and draws a deep breath. He looks down at the newspaper in his hands, stares at it briefly, then lets it flutter to the floor. He exits as the lights fade.*)


*The curtain falls.*

# PRODUCTION INFORMATION

# PERFORMANCE AGREEMENT

1. *Troubled House* is © 2003 Daniel Schwabauer and may not be presented without the written permission of the author. You must purchase playbooks for your cast, production and backstage staff, unless other written arrangements are made with the author. Multiple copies are available at a discounted rate when used for production. It is a violation of federal copyright law and international treaties to reproduce copyrighted material, in any form, without the written permission of the copyright owner.

2. Whenever *Troubled House* is presented in any form (full-production, limited production, staged-reading, etc.), at any level (equity, non-equity, community theater, college, school, etc.), whether by amateurs or professionals, the following notices must appear on all related printed materials including programs, advertising, etc.: "Produced by special arrangement with the author" and "www.troubledhouse.com." Furthermore, the author must be fully credited on all such materials.

3. A production photo and a copy of all playbills, programs, print advertising, and reviews must be sent to the author at the end of the production run agreed to in this license.

4. Royalties are due automatically whether or not admission is charged if any spectator observes the play, including parents or other classes not involved with the production. Royalties for amateur productions (community theater, college, high school, etc.) are due in advance. This performance agreement will be considered invalid if royalty payments and a signed copy of this contract are not received by the author prior to the performance. Guarantee of performance dates cannot be secured until royalty payments are received. For pricing of playbooks, royalty application or other information, visit the website or contact the author at: dan@troubledhouse.com.

*Thank you for your interest in producing* Troubled House*! It is my desire to help you make your production as easy and as rewarding as possible. Please feel free to contact me with questions or comments regarding my work.*

www.troubledhouse.com

distributed by :

Clear Water Press
PO Box 62
Olathe, KS 66051
www.clearwaterpress.com

www.ingramcontent.com/pod-product-compliance
Lightning Source LLC
Chambersburg PA
CBHW031321040426
42443CB00005B/176